DATE DUE

PICASSO

and the BULL

VINCENTE MARRERO Suárez

Translated by

ANTHONY KERRIGAN

HENRY REGNERY COMPANY ❧ *Chicago* ❧ *1956*

PROLOGUE

THE OBJECT of this work is the interpretation of a number of paintings by Picasso on the same theme: the myth of the bull. The author has thought it advisable to precede the study with an introduction and to follow it with an epilogue, his only pretension being to situate the work of the artist in his ambient. It [illegible]d have been a pleasure to state at this point: at the center are the paintings, and here are the interpretations. But it could not be. Nothing is more rebellious than a painting of Picasso in the face of a definite statement, of any certain (or even half-certain) interpretation. Yet, the author of this monograph has been brazen enough. . . .

But in treating of painting, it is not enough to "read, read, and then . . . be brazen," as a Russian poet recommends. Besides, it is necessary to look, to look a good deal,

 Library of Congress Catalog Card Number 56:11852.

Originally published as *Picasso y el toro* by Vicente Marrero Suarez, by Editorial Calamo, Madrid, n.d.

the subject of Picasso there is an absolute scarcity of interpretation, and, where there is interpretation, there is a dearth of the monograph. On a theme as central to his work as the myth of the bull there is not, to my knowledge, a single study. And so, the author of such a study, necessarily a Spaniard, here offers his services.

and to know how to look. Pictorial interpretations are allowed only in front of the canvas, while looking. And if there is anything clear in these days, it is that we have paid scant attention to the *gift* of interpretation; and this is due, probably, to the method of interpretation inherited from the past century, a century so self-possessed, so rationalist and so convinced of its method. That century was too disrespectful to be a good interpreter. To interpret is to go to school to another spirit, not so as to set it in order, but to learn; not to judge it, but to open it up to our sensibility without doing it the violence which customarily accompanies our own ideas; and not to locate it within the orbit of our own being, but rather to amplify our own limits. Plato can not be read—as he frequently was a few years ago—with the idea in mind of subjecting his ideas to whatever system of thought is preferred by the reader. For this very reason the Neo-Kantian view of Plato demanded revision. Every epoch adopts its own attitude concerning the past; what is truly surprising is to find people who not only are not prepared to consider, to *listen,* but who also have decided and predetermined the way in which previous generations acted or should have acted. Perhaps this is the reason that every epoch rewrites, must rewrite, past history.

Strangely enough, in all the mountain of writing on

CONTENTS

"L'homme passe infiniment l'homme."

PASCAL, *Pensées.*

"Ce n'est pas d'après nature que je travaille, mais devant la nature, avec elle."

PROPOS DE PICASSO À TERIADE.
Intransegeant. 1932.

". . . just as if we came from an eminently poetic, philosophic, and musical time and wanted to enter into one which was decidedly visual."

"Art does not need friends, enjoyers, connoisseurs or critics, so much as it does those who will look upon it with respect and veneration."

PINDER.
Von den Künsten und der Kunst, 17, 77.

ILLUSTRATIONS

Representations of the Bull

ANIMAL of mystery, horned enigma, the bull for centuries has figured in the profoundest myths of man. And men still fight bulls in the *plazas de toros* and men still dream the dreams of myth. In the eyes of those who understand the ritual it is clear that over and above all human considerations lies the myth and the mystery. The inhuman, anti-human, aspect of the animal, the enigma, the "otherness" are qualities which led primitive peoples to consider it the bearer of power, all-powerful. Only gradually did the belief die down. Then, from something like a mixture of fear, shame, and reflection the cult of the animal was born; the cult involved a feeling which is not easy for us to understand, and yet we can appreciate it. If we consider what the running of the bulls means for the Spanish even today, we see that the bull is an exception to all the existing relations which have grown up between men and animals.

What then must be the special character of this ruminant, short-haired mammal? At one time or another it has been possessed of a sacred character in a great part of the world. In Egypt, in Vedic India, Babylonia, Crete, across the Mediterranean. One need only recall the minotaur, the taurobolia, the Mithraic cult. It was a sacrificial animal among the Indo-Aryans as it was among the Jews. On Roman friezes, Bueranius-garlanded appeared with frequency. Guardian of the occult, symbol of procreation, of Dionysus, of St. Luke the Evangelist, of the Borgias. The oldest solar sign in the zodiac, and in the world of spoken Spanish still the sign of a tellurian spontaneity. In the afternoons of ancient Spanish towns, after the harvest is brought in, to mark the splendor or the penury of the grain, there is the running of the bulls, just as in the finest of the provincial capitals. Great rings filled with colors and voices, and the grace of the actors in the drama, the guards and the provocative colors, the fans and Havana cigars, the elegance of dress and the pomp, a luminous exaltation, a rhythmic and poetic libation offered in black blood.

> The fabric of the heavens matched
> and folded into separate bolts,
> a sash reverberating sun:
> the Spanish amphitheatre's gyve
> 's a zodiac of symbols come alive.

Thus did the bullring appear to Calderón, with his habitual sense of the stunning. Or, as Lope de Vega would have it:

> Now the plaza's hung
> with tapestry and pansy:
> a thousand women at the windows,
> and at each one a heaven hangs.

"Che volete? é uno spettacolo selvaggio, ma é il piu grandioso di tutti gli spettacoli dell' epoca nostra. . . ." A spectacle possessed of grace, gesture, garb, a content and a context such as even the antique world did not possess.

But, and it must be admitted at once, the Spanish fiesta contains as great a mystery as misunderstanding of what it entails. The truths of the bullfight are no longer to be found in the theories and opinions which have been stirred up by the contest, but in the art of painting. We have here chosen painting as the shortest, most certain, and perhaps least complicated road by which to reach the dark quintessence of the Spanish fiesta. Pictorial art has always been representative not only of epochs but of the various attitudes of men, of different ways of "looking at things." In a world as eminently visual as ours, so satiated with letters, it will serve us well.

Among the painters we will be satisfied with Picasso.

Until his appearance on the scene, painters had been losing themselves in details whenever they dealt with the corrida. Former painters have been carried away by the anecdotal, the illustrative, or the colorful, elements which, if they are not exactly false, are beside the point. The most famous representation of the fiesta, the *Tauromaquia* series of Goya, does not go beyond the limits of masterful illustration. It is a description, a graphic manual of the ways and manners of displaying courage, of risking one's life, of feats of prowess which are sometimes actually alien to the spirit of the bullfight. Spectacular facets, popular anecdote side by side with epical celebration, bitter analogy mixed with melancholia, and bulls whose outlines are too prettily perfect or too puffed with pride. Though the marvelous plastic movement of the drawings surpasses the forms themselves, and the artist's immediacy of perception overcomes the very solidity of the figures, the *Tauròmaquia* of Goya is simply a study, which in no way plumbs the ultimate vision of the corrida, despite the fact that Goya, as Baudelaire said, *"plein de choses inconnues,"* achieved impossible feats.

About Manet and his school, something of the same nature can be said. Manet was, next to the Aragonese Goya, the painter who has established the rules for looking at the bullfight. French *"gaieté"* kept Manet and his school from the bitter and painful tone which marked

Goya's work. There is little in Manet's art of the Spaniard's fascination with the far-fetched, the hallucinatory, the polyp-headed mob, the amorphous multitude. Manet, who nevertheless grew to be passionately interested in Goya, preferred to paint the masses of live variegated color by means of simple daubs representing the expectant multitudes heaped in the stone rows of the amphitheatre. He attempts only to reflect the warm, luminous ambient, the atmosphere radiant with color, by an infinitude of chromatic notes across the surface of the canvas: the bullfighter's "suit of lights," the blinding plethora of hues, circles of sun and shade. Like Bizet's *Carmen* all this sets everybody's blood on fire—except the Spaniard's. In this Impressionist school, the abundance of light and color is out of proportion to the line and the form which traces and suggests the depth of the spectacle. The black crape, the antique embroidery of heavy gold, the short jackets of gold-thread, the black torero hats and the pinnacled head-ribbons of the matador, the silken sashes, baize pants and spurs, girt chinstraps around swaggerer's faces . . . none of this is untrue, but there is much left unseen by French impressionist painting, to whom the Spanish fiesta nevertheless owes a debt of gratitude.

But we are not dealing here with the question of styles. As long as the style corresponds to the reality and depth of the corrida, any style is acceptable. So that it is not the aim here to entertain ourselves with such painters as Zuloaga and Vázquez Díaz, who are more exactly portrait painters of torerors than painters of the corrida as such, or with such painters of provincial fiestas in the ancient towns of Castille as Solana. As splendid as these painters often are, their work falls outside the limits of our subject. Even the painters of posters or of fans have their place, though it is not in this essay, as do the *avant-garde* painters whose works now appear in the official salons and whose painting is more in the nature of allegorical allusion than plastic representation of living reality. Picasso is a case apart, and that is our theme.

The Bull in Ancient Myth

IN ORDER to explain the vision of the bull which is Picasso's, it will be of value to outline the role of the bull in ancient myth and the intimate relationship existing between the myth and the present Spanish corrida. Without this explanation it would not be possible to understand the painter's unique gift.

We must make one assumption: the Spanish fiesta is something more than color, emotion, grace, strong sensations. It should be obvious to anyone at first glance that for the Spaniard the corrida is far from being a mere sport, or a fight at all, such as is suggested by the inaccuracies of the translation of the word "corrida" into foreign languages, and of which the English "bullfight" is a good example of distortion. The corrida is much more than a *"stierkampf"* or a "bullfight." The struggle between man and beast is an element of the corrida, but what raises the spirit of the *aficionado* is not the battle itself, or the prowess displayed, as is vulgarly thought outside of Spain. Rather, in the corrida the Spaniard seeks class, grace, form, expertness, elegance, and above all, mastery and dominion as an end in itself. The element of risk as such is admitted (and then with reservations) only in the most savage fiestas. The corrida is art and fete, and also something serious, with a certain tragic and crepuscular air about it, despite the richness of the color with which the Spanish always deck the plaza. In sum, it is the least profane of profane spectacles. The very joy of a *pasodoble* heard outside of Spain by a Spaniard contains for him the seriousness and anguish which are part of the fiesta. The atmosphere and enthusiasm of the plaza, unlike that in any recreation or revel, has about it something profound and mysterious. The ambient of a corrida is heavy with occult suggestion, a quality that Picasso has divined.

In Spain in the 19th century there was a prevalent influence which strove despotically to clarify everything, and which, sometimes with incisive appropriateness on the part of the authorities charged with regulating public spectacles, regulated the corrida from top to bottom with rules and authoritarian edicts which were often more proper to French mentalities than Spanish: not one banderilla, but a pair; three picks, three pairs. . . . Despite this rationalizing tendency, the original mystery has not ceased to animate the fiesta.

The mythical evolves and enriches itself. One myth survives, another is completely transformed, an older one reappears. The figure of Mithra has a bearing on the representation of Christ as a spiritual Sun. The symbolism of the solstice has affected the Christian festival of Christmas. The figure of Hercules looms behind St. George and the dragon. There is no lack of examples. In story and in fable myths are deprived of their seriousness and given a frivolous and amusing character; but they maintain their serious aspect in those areas of the *psyche* where the dominion of thought or of the conscious will does not extend, an area which remains beyond them; in short, in the sphere of the spontaneous.[1] This is a fact we should not forget in dealing with the corrida. An overly abstract or aesthetic concept of myth, taken from the books of classical mythology, has prevented us from divining the persistence of myth in the modern world. In any case, myth is not so much a matter of meditation as an actuality, a reiteration of potent

[1] *Vide* C. G. Jung and K. Kerényi, *Einführung in das Wesen der Mythologie,* 1941, III, p. 25; and G. van der Leeuw, *Phänomenologie der Religion,* 1939, p. 60.

events not only in words, but in forms. Myth does not take the shape of earthly reality, but rather does the figure of myth shape reality itself.

In order to understand the world of myths it would be wise not to take as point of departure our present level of consciousness, illustrated as it is by science and confirmed by technology, nor is it best to start from any abstraction, especially in view of the way, as Guardini has said, "myths have been elbowed into the street." For the primitive world, existence was made up of powers; relationships were not comprehended scientifically in concepts and theories, but rather felt intuitively in images and symbols, products of rudimentary intelligence, which appeared when primitive people strove to participate in or understand something not immediately apperceivable. Whatever was recounted, whatever was listened to, whatever was lived through, was represented, and symbolically executed in the ritual of the cult, and thus did primitive men deal with existence and with themselves.

Myth is the *"sancta simplicitas"* of the human race. It knows no time; its magical *now* is not a *mere* now; it is not simply a moment, a singular present, but is, in the expression of Leibniz: "charged with the past and heavy with the future."

The gods and demons encountered in primitive societies are personifications, the vivification of collective desires, *"le desir collectif personifié,"* and the themes of myth and its ritual acts are infinitely variable, incalculable, unfathomable. The motivations of mythic thought and imagination are, in a certain sense, always the same: in the sense that we find a "certain unity in diversity, within the different activities of human culture." In the same way that art offers us a unity of intuition, and that science offers us a unity of method, so does myth offer us its special unity; something distinct from emotion, a collective expression and an objectification of man's social experience.[2]

One of the myths most widely extended among primitive peoples is the myth of the light and the dark. It is this myth which lives on in Picasso and is the key to his vision of the corrida.

Primitive man viewed the darkness, not only as impenetrable and dangerous, but as an evil and terrifying force. The fear which even today a child feels is not caused by anything palpable or definite. Darkness is a force in itself. At dawn the sun rises, and light, its benevolent attribute, vanquishes the dark, whereupon man takes new courage. Existence was forcibly subordinated to two forces, darkness and light. Light came from

[2] *Vide* Ernest Cassirer, *The Myth of the State,* 1946, p. 54.

the sun and was divine, a divinity. But the Sun God was engaged in a continuing battle. Each morning he rose from the sea, vanquished the darkness and reigned throughout the day; but at dusk, darkness again triumphed and gradually regained possession of the world. Alongside this struggle which went on day after day there developed another war which was waged through the year: toward the middle of winter the sun was utterly weakened; thereafter, it began to gain strength, its light became clearer, its rays became warmer, its arc was raised and the day grew longer. This was considered to be a victory of the Sun God over the power of darkness, and the day of the solstice was one of mysterious triumph. But then, after the summer solstice, the sacred arc once again went into a decline. The force of heat and of light diminished, the darkness and the cold increased and seemed on the point of supremacy. Ignorant of the laws of nature, primitive man lived the struggle in a direct manner, trembling lest the sun remain forever vanquished by the darkness. And thus was born the myth of the light and darkness. Light was embodied in the Sun God, the radiant, ardent being replete with all the power of life and prosperity. Darkness was embodied in the dragon, the snake, the wolf Fenris, a being who inspired terror and breathed death. The victory of the Sun God and of the Dragon alternated. Some myths manifest a presentiment that the Sun will one day perish: the Dragon will definitively triumph, the wolf Fenris will devour the Sun, and thus will all things end.[3] In these pessimistic presentiments of the primitive mentality lies the true antecedents of Picasso.

The subject of interest to us in this myth of light and darkness is the part played by the bull in the ritual of the solar myths. As the Frenchman Douté said, the rites persist though the creeds change, like the fossils of those

[3] *Vide* Romano Guardini, *Der Heilbringer in Mythos*, 1946, Chapter 1. Some well-known investigators, Max Müller for example, consider all extant myths to be variants of the myth of light and darkness, the basis of all other myths. This belief is nowadays thought too dogmatic and is not shared in the most recent investigations on mythology. In his day, Max Müller found a similarity between the Greek legends of Selene and Endymion, Eos and Tityus, Cephalus and Procris, Daphne and Apollo. According to this investigator, all these symbolic personages were variations of the same myth endlessly repeated: the rise and setting of the sun, the battle between the light and the dark. Each new myth represents the same phenomenon in a new and different perspective. Endymion, for example, is not the Sun in its divine character as Phoebus, but a concept of the sun in its daily course, emerging early from the womb of Aurora and submerging late, after a rapid and brilliant career, never to return to mortal life. And what else might Daphne be, pursued by Apollo, but Aurora hastening precipitately across the sky and disappearing before the sudden apparition of the brilliant sun? The same with the legend of the death of Hercules. The tunic which Deyanira sends the solar hero represents her visualization of the clouds which rise from the waters and envelop the sun like a dark vestment. Hercules attempts to divest himself of it, but can not do so without dismembering his own body; finally, his radiant essence is consumed in a general conflagration. *Vide* Max Müller, *Comparative Mythology*, Oxford Essays, p. 52.

extinct molluscs which serve to date geologic epochs. Ideas and symbolic representations are not the only elements manifested in rituals. It has been said that if myth is the epic element of primitive religious life, the rites are the dramatic element. The question of which of these two elements is first and which is second can not be posed; neither exists separately, without relation or interdependence, but rather do they complement and explain each other.

For our purposes it will suffice to point out the importance of the bull in solar ritual. Avoiding any reference to oriental cultures, or the role played by the bull as a transitional element between oriental and occidental cultures, we will limit ourselves to the bull in the mythic past of the Mediterranean. From Heliopolis and ancient Memphis, center of the adoration of the bull Ra and the ox Apis, through Crete, where archeological discoveries have revealed that tauromachic activities (taurotenias and taurocatapsias) in the Greek world harkened back to a great antiquity, and as far as Acci, today called Guadix, the entire *mare nostrum* is one single symbolic taurine skin of dark color. Nîmes carries the magical beast sculptured on its stones. Artemis, who emigrated to Tauris mounted on a bull, was the patroness of Massilia (Marseilles), of Antipolis (Antibes), of Arelate (Arles), of Nemausus (Nîmes). Diodorus of Sicily speaks of the sacred character of the bull in Spain.

There are evocative legends of all sorts, from the taurobolius in the religion of Mithra to the voyage of Hercules.

The majority of modern mythologists see in the Minotaur a solar personification. In Cook's discussion of the Minotaur[4] he points out that studies in Cretan mythology seem to show that the sun was considered to be like a bull and that in the rites proper to the island the labyrinth was a kind of "orchestra," based on a solar model, in which there took place a mimetic dance. The dancer who represented the sun dressed in the costume of a bull. In Cnossus the hereditary prince wore the mask of a bull, thus proclaiming the divine or solar character of his person. The Roman dances called Trojans, which were popularized throughout Europe, were known to have taurine elements. The battle with the Minotaur was an event which was used over and over again in ceramic painting, especially on containers decorated with black figures; the chăracteristic pose showed the hero armed with a sword and dragging the Minotaur out of the labyrinth.

And does not Mithra, the god of light, the genius of celestial illumination, always appear before us in full daylight, ever awake and prepared, observing with careful eye and ready to respond to the call of the weak,

[4] *Vide* Cook, *Zeus, p.* 490.

battling by night against shadows and blackness and by day against clouds and dark squalls, and traversing the firmament mounted on a chariot drawn by four fiery white horses? In graphic art Mithra is represented as a heroic figure of cosmogony, being born from behind rocks like a sun shining over a hilltop, or is shown in battle with the mythological bull. Thus, too, the crypts and subterranean recesses where the cult of Mithra was celebrated were commonly decorated with a relief showing Mithra in the act of killing the mythic bull. On the fete days dedicated to Mithra, copious libations were drunk, solemn sacrifices were offered and there were large-scale ceremonies. The Mithrakanas were famous, but Mithraism, despite its large sphere of influence, never achieved status as an official religion and always conserved its private mysteries.

There are examples, it is true, of ancient myths in which the bull is looked upon as the personification of light, of good. But in any case, the role it plays is always relevant to the myth of light and dark.

Statues of Mithra, represented at the moment of vanquishing the bull, whose death is to bring in its train a multitude of benefits for humanity, have been found in Spain, a memorial of Spanish integration into the Roman Empire. Professor García Bellido has studied these elements of Spanish archeology in recent works devoted to the infiltration into the Latin world of religious ideas from all parts of the Empire, most singularly from the Orient (dating from the beginning of the second century B.C.), and of their entrenchment in the most hidden and recondite corners of society. Numerous creeds were cultivated simultaneously, sometimes independently one of another, often in a parasitical manner, under the protection of the official Roman religion; they all lived together in harmony, without rivalries or invidious suspicion of the gods in the Graeco-Roman pantheon. Of all the cults, the one which spread with the greatest rapidity, making millions of proselytes all over the known world, was the cult of the Persian god Mithra. Perhaps its success was due to the fact that it was the only religion coming from Iran which provided for representational figures. The triumph of Mithraism is all the more remarkable in that its deity was native to a country traditionally the enemy of Rome. The religion had first taken hold among the soldiers fighting against the Persians on the Mesopotamian frontiers; it then spread through the armies, to all the frontiers of the Empire where the Roman legions were posted on guard against barbarian incursion. During the second and third centuries of our era, the cult of Mithra was almost universal in the army, and outside it as well. Christianity was passing through the hardest tests. It was miraculous that Mithraism should have suffered an almost total eclipse quickly and through the agency of Christianity, despite the fact that the latter had arrayed against it the powerful machinery of the Roman state, with all the resources of repression and persecution at its disposal. Still, the triumph of Christianity notwithstanding, some shred of Mithraism still survived at the beginning of the fourth century. And even today, there are many subterranean currents flowing into Europe from Asia which can count on the basic foundation of a dualist theogony, neither Trinitarian nor Christian, propagated long ago in the soul of the West, and once incorporated in such religions as Mithraism.[5]

In May of 1952, in the fields near Cabra, a splendid town of the Cordova region, along the Guadalquivir river in southern Spain, there was unearthed one of those Mithraic images which represent a bull overthrown and sprawled on the ground in his death throes, while a young hero on horseback leans down, though his eyes are turned to the sky, to thrust a wide knife into the beast's neck. Probably dating from the second century of the present era, it is now one of the most interesting

[5] The question of the relation between Christianity and Mithraism is a hotly debated one, and completely unresolved. A work like that of K. Prümm, *Religionsgeschichtliches Handbuch für den Raum der altchristlichen Umwelt*, 1943, p. 282, leaves open even the degree to which Mithraism was a rival to the propagation of Christianity. A syncretic religion, situated between Indo-Germanic mythology and Persian dualism, Mithraism never was widely diffused in Spain, despite the traces remaining there.

pieces in the Archeological Museum of Cordova. The Mithraic sanctuary at Mérida is also known to date from the second century. From San Juan de la Isla there has come another Mithraic relic in Spain, a stone with the text of a Mithraic prayer inscribed. It is interesting to note that, although the cult of Mithra was not as widely diffused in Spain as it was in the frontier regions of the Roman Empire (the reason for this being that there was only one permanent legion stationed in Spain), nevertheless, this cult prospered in the south of the Iberian peninsula, between the Guadiana and the Guadalquivir rivers, that is, in the regions most purely devoted, nowadays as well as historically, to the bullfight.[6]

Still, of all the cults whose influence was extended through the Western Roman Empire the one proportionally the worst represented, or, more exactly, the one with the least density of occurrence within the Iberian peninsula, is the cult of Mithra. In his great work on the Iranian divinity, published in 1899, Cumont pointed out this unique status: "Spain is the poorest country of the entire West in Mithraic monuments." And García Bellido, in his recent studies on the cult in Spain, and after half a century of chance finds in the fields, which

[6] This fact is made clear in the map on "Mithraism in Hispania" made by García Bellido, in his *La península Iberica en los comienzos de su historia,* 1953; and especially in the chapter "Un rival de Cristo en España: Mithras," p. 555.

have not, however, added greatly to the primitive and precarious list, has not substantially modified Cumont's judgment. As already mentioned, this phenomenon is easily explained by the generally pacific state of Spain in the second and third centuries, which precluded the need for occupation forces of numerous garrisons, that is, contact with the main carrier of Mithraism.[7] But there is enough material on hand to allow of the making of hypotheses to help clarify in some ways "the lost origins in remote times." To suppose that the Spanish national fiesta is an ancient Hispanic institution which precedes all known invasions of the peninsula, does not take away from the mythic content of the bull; on the contrary, proofs exist which point to the sacred character of the bull on Spanish soil.

Among the Chilcotiis Indians, when an eclipse occurs, the men dance in a circle to help the sun in the sickness which they think it is undergoing at the moment. The dance of Ariadne, in more ancient times, was an imitation of the passage of the day-star across the sky, something in the nature of assistance rendered by sympathetic magic to aid the sun in its course. And in Egypt, the pharaoh, who was considered to be the earthly representative of the sun, solemnly danced around the

[7] A. García y Bellido, "El Culto de Mithras en la península Ibérica," *Boletín de la Real Academia de la Historia,* CXXII, (1948) p. 293.

walls of the temple with the aim of assisting the sun in its movements overhead. The same principles of sympathetic magic existed in Spain, and, as occurs in all cultures, these principles gradually were integrated into other superior, analogous forms brought by the numerous invaders of Spain.[8]

From the most remote prehistoric epochs there are vestiges of a cult, combining utilitarianism and myth, which the primitive inhabitants rendered to the bull as well as to the horse. Traces of the cult are also found in coins, which reflect the customs and myths of the people who mint them. A numismatic exposition in Madrid in 1951 featured a display of 320 coins with representations

[8] As regards Spain, the thesis continues to be upheld, as by McKennan in *Paganism and Pagan Survivals in Spain up to the Fall of the Visigothic Kingdom* (Washington, 1938), that the early forms of popular and indigenous religions survived despite later invasions of the Peninsula. The same thesis is defended by G. Drieux in his *Cultes indigenes de Ligons* (Paris, 1934), when he says that the mass of the people, the *civitas* of Langres, assimilated Gallico-Roman culture only in small measure and passed directly from the indigenous religion to Christianity. For the comprehension of the bull in its ultimate antecedents and significance, it is necessary to note that the Celts already knew the three-horned bull, the bull-river symbol, and other representations of the taurine mysteries. Not without reason has Altheim written, in his *Italia und Rom* (Amsterdam, 1941), that "a great kingdom, that of the divine bulls, extends across the Mediterranean world from Asia Minor to Spain"; and Altheim ventures the supposition that Rome suppressed the Italic cult of the bull, because numerous renegade groups fought against her beneath this sign.

of bulls and horses. The figure of the bull is characteristic of ancient Spanish coins, both as a result of Cretan influence, as Schulten suggests, and because of a veneration of the bull as an element in the common mythological instinct. The Iberians wore amulets in the form of a bull, and in general, as can be seen from their prehistoric monuments, the inhabitants of the entire peninsula rendered this animal some form of homage. In the Balearic islands the bronze bulls' heads of Costix are still to be seen; and the study of coins makes clear the relation of the bull with the half-moon, a relationship touched on by Strabo: "The Celts and other nations contiguous with them in the north have a certain nameless divinity to which family groups render homage in the name of the full-moon, by dancing in front of their houses until dawn." Certain Graeco-Roman influences are manifested in the coins of the Balearic island of Ibiza and the city of Sagunto (Roman *Saguntum*) on the east coast of Spain—the first well-defined coins on which the bull appears. The most perfect example of Spanish numismatics remains the mitred bull of Caesar-Augustus: a strong standing wild bull, image of power, reproduced on the coins of many regions, where all the mythological symbolism of the bull assumes an expression utterly contrasting with the gentle pastoral submission of the yoked plowing bulls which appear on other coins. The horse, also, appears on the first Spanish coins; and the image of Pegasus, introduced by the Greeks at Ampurias in the fifth century, changes its Greek inscriptions to Iberian epigraphs.[9]

Today, there are numerous disciplines and beliefs which impel us to concern ourselves more intimately with the totemic animal than with the modern "spectacle," whatever the origins of the latter: we are led in this direction by the modern studies on myth, by the current sociology and phenomenology of religion, by psychoanalysis, by a greater knowledge of the structure of the corrida and of art history, and by the marvelous and instinctual element of Christianity which we still study separately. The bloodthirsty contests of the Roman arena, or the hunts staged in the amphitheatres are too modern to serve as points of departure for study of the origins of the Spanish fiesta, though it is most tempting to trace the beginnings of the bullfight to the Roman games. Covarrubias is one of those who believe that the Romans introduced tauromaquia into Spain, but the terrain in this area of speculation is too unstable underfoot to allow of pontification and final answers. In any case, there are no documents to substantiate the affirmation that the tauromaquia of the Roman epoch was linked with the games of the Aegean world, and the two spectacles present notable differences. The presence of the horse in the Roman games may perhaps liken it to the spectacles of Thessalonic Greece more than to

[9] José de Yriarte, "Caballos y toros en la numismática hispánica," *Archivo Español de Arqueologia,* XXV (1952) p.134.

those of Aegean Greece, since it appears that in the time of Claudius horsemen from Thessalonica battled in the Roman circus against wild bulls; though it is true also that the bull played a role in the hunting celebrations which took place in the amphitheatres.

Sharing the opinion of Covarrubias in regard to the immediate history of the corrida is one of the greatest authorities on Hispanic historiography, Father Mariana; in his *Tratado contra los juegos públicos o de espectáculos* (Treatise Against Public Games or Spectacles—whose twentieth chapter is titled "What is the origin of the corrida?") he holds that the Spanish fiesta is a remnant of the complex of spectacles which "were anciently used at Rome, and which from that city, as from a fountain, were poured out on the provinces."[10]

As already stated, the civilizations of the Mediter-

[10] These games belong, without doubt, writes Father Mariana, to the ancient genus of spectacles which in Latin were called *manus*, so-called because, as Tertulian says in his book *On Spectacles* (Ch. XII), they represent an office, and the ancients thought that in this spectacle an office or service for the dead was carried out. The gladiators, likewise, fought for the honor of the dead and attempted to placate with their blood the dead souls, whom they called *manes*. The taurine games were anciently held in the Circus Flaminius and were dedicated to the infernal gods, with the aim of placating the souls of the dead. There were times, according to Sixtus Pompeius, when so many bulls were killed that new-born children died of the overwhelming odor. The games originated, says Father Mariana, from idolatry; Constantine suppressed the law of the Gladiatoribus, whereupon the games passed out of existence.

ranean, whether expressed in Greek or Roman myth, displayed a constant fascination with the image of the bull, a fascination not devoid of mystic admiration. And it is noteworthy that this concern with the bull possessed not only a religious and mythic significance, but that even in antiquity this fascination had been degraded and the taurine games had been converted into a mere spectacle or a game of profane characteristics. The ceremony of beheading the bulls, which originally appeared in conjunction with the taurobolius, or bull hunts, were baptisms of blood in which the death of the bull was accompanied by a simulation of the hunt. The animal, after being released in the field, was apprehended by the faithful and sacrificed by means of a special dagger; its blood, still warm, was then gathered and poured over the head of the initiate. The taurobolius were generally celebrated for the health of the Emperor. The last example of these ceremonies known in Spain dates from 390; it is in the simulated hunt which precedes the decollation that the antecedents of the modern bullfight are thought to reside. But alongside the taurobolius, and this is where the discussion was leading us, are the taurocholia and the taurokathapsia, of the Hellenistic and Roman epoch, and these are purely games, athletic spectacles more than sacrifices, in which the animal did not run the fatal risk. Many monuments of antiquity reproduce scenes taken from these games; frescoes and stone carvings represent them as gymnastic exercises carried out to demonstrate the dexterity and audacity of the participating athlete. Reichel, amplifying the studies of Mayer describes how the man runs to encounter the animal, and after seizing the horns, throws it to the ground or jumps upon its back. These contests were diffused over a wide area, and may have had a religious origin which they had since lost.

In any case, the idea is completely discredited today that "lance and tourney are the Moor's contagion," as Quevedo believed. No Arabic text mentions either, but rather it is the texts of *Moriscos,* of Moors in Spain after the reconquest, which do.

The Spanish corrida lends itself to so much speculation and to so many possible theories—many of them ingenuous in the extreme—that a work of such a fundamental nature as Cossío's declines to deal with most of them.[11] Nevertheless, there is much valuable material to be found in taurine bibliography, as for instance, in the works of the Marquis of San Juan de Piedras Albas. Among other problems of a fruitful nature which occur to this author, as he studies the corrida in the old laws and statutes, is the one of how the ancient legislators and rulers of Spain looked upon the corrida; for example, what reasoning impelled Alfonso the Wise in his *Par-*

[11] *Vide* also his article "De los orígenes de las fiestas de toros," *El Ruedo,* May, 1944.

tidas to consider the profession of bullfighting to be infamous. Does this proscription relate to the spirit behind the laws punishing those "*qui nocturna sacrificia dasantibus celebrant,*" laws bearing on the nocturnal celebrations in Spain in the sixth century? Some Spanish provinces still preserve the cult of the bull of San Marcos, one of many instances of how the indigenous cult was grafted on to Christianity, preserving meanwhile its proper characteristics and customs. Finally, tournaments and bulls were basic ingredients in the life of play in the Middle Ages.

If we avoid taking the space to record again the words of the chroniclers regarding the first knight to contend with a bull, the Cid Campeador, whom Goya himself presents in the act of placing the lance in the eleventh plate of his *Tauromaquia,* nevertheless, we can scarcely leave unmentioned the fiesta which the Licentiate Francisco de Cepeda speaks of in his "*Resumpta historial de España,*" a fiesta of nobility which took place in 1100: the author adds that this type of fete was peculiar to the Spanish nation. It is recorded in the chronicles that on the occasion of the marriage of Alfonso VII and Doña Berenguela, at Saldaña in 1124, taurine celebrations were held. And the same type of festival marked the marriage ceremony between the daughter of Alfonso VIII and García, King of Navarre.

For a Spaniard, there is nothing surprising in the fact

that a holy pope like Pius V was powerless to halt the Spanish fiesta during the years in which his prohibitive papal edict was in force. For his part even Francisco de Vitoria assured Philip II that the fiesta was not illicit. Already years before, in 1493, Queen Isabella the Catholic had responded negatively to her confessor Fray Hernando de Talavera, who was attempting to influence her to forbid the fiesta: "This is not something which has to do with me alone," was her sage reply.

In the 18th century, after the decadence of the bullfight from horseback, unmounted fighting comes into prominence, especially in Andalucía. A curious question is inevitable at this point: how explain the sudden flowering of the corrida in which the great number of the active participants were people from the lower classes? May not this phenomenon make it appear that the knights were intruders in the festivals of bulls, as a result of a very Spanish tendency to mix the noble with the popular, and the grandiose with the picaresque? It is surprising that the first written report that we have of the taurine festivals in the Middle Ages indicates that they are already royal celebrations. Does this not presuppose a previously fixed and rooted tradition? On this very question of the antiquity of the unmounted bullfight, Rodríguez Marín[12] suggests a modification of the

[12] *Vide Felipe II, tauróphilo.*

date which is commonly used for the point of origin, inasmuch as at the Council of Osuna (1584) an order was given "to run four bulls, four 'bulls of the cape.'" In Spain there have always been skillful men dedicated to carrying out the various roles called for in the celebration of the corrida.

All these observations are made in the interest of establishing the importance of myth in the corrida and of its possible survival in time. Myths evolve from one place to another, suffer corruption of various sorts and change their primitive character, but may, all the while, conserve something of their inner structure.

The Corrida Today

THE VERY STRUCTURE of the corrida dictates that it be played out on more levels than on the visual level alone. Before us is an animal which must be reduced and brought to submission. The aesthetics of the corrida is not a personal matter, an artist's aesthetic alone, but must develop in relation to the effect made on the animal. "It is not a matter of ballet, in which, once visual aesthetic is attained, the greater part of the spectacle's aim is achieved. The corrida, despite its visual aesthetics, would not reach a positive eventuation were it not for the *faena,* the capework, which achieves the purpose of overcoming the bull psychologically, and this is true, whatever the misunderstanding and uninformed applause of the spectators." In its own way and at its own level, the corrida has all the formal characteristics of an ethical action, so that its formal structure is closely related to something religious, mythical.

We already know that for the mass of people, who are necessarily simple, ingenuous, placid, the spectacle is sheer diversion. And we know that when the minority speak with depreciation of "fighting for the Gallery" or of an "offering to the sun," they indicate discontent with a torero who shows little scruple and makes use of false tricks—minimum merit and over-apparent courage—, while the phrases by implication also question the public's understanding, which often does not go beyond appreciation of the spectacular. In any case, "it is one thing to fight the bull, and another to make passes with a cape or a muleta," a celebrated contemporary Spanish torero has said with lapidary precision recently.[13] When, in a corrida, there is capework in which twenty, thirty, forty passes are made, and still the animal retains its vigor and integrity, then, at the moment of the kill the torero will either be hugging the walls, or he will strike bone in the animal or he will unskillfully run him through with the sword to no avail. If and when this happens, despite the great number of passes which went before, passes of apparent beauty to the great public, the bull has not been brought to submission and the torero has not triumphed; he has not even finished his work.

In its present form the corrida offers an accumulation of significant suggestions; yet, practically and concretely

[13] Domingo Ortega, in his *El Arte del Toreo,* with an appendix by José Ortega y Gasset (Madrid, 1950).

it is impossible to point out the relation which exists between the present corrida and the antique myth. The appearance of the victor, the saviour, in the myth or in the corrida, is a deeply moving moment. The instant he appears, it is known, it is felt, that he possesses superior power. Dispenser of fortune, he inundates the plaza with enthusiasm. The figure who battles is almost always the central figure of myth: and he pays for his victory with his life, which culminates in his act of salvation. The mythical deed assumes a destruction the like of which occurs in the corrida. And he who understands the myth, understands the act of salvation, and penetrates to the complex of the undertaking.

The forms and the dress which survive in the corrida are today enigmatic. If many of their archtypes can be discovered in the centuries immediately preceding, it is nevertheless always surprising to note the ease and facility with which they are accepted in the modern tauromaquia. And these forms and this dress contribute greatly to the identification of the corrida with ritual.

Blood and breath are the principal elements in all rites. And blood there is in the bullfight: too much for many people, though "the purple blood is agreeable in the eyes of the gods." The breath is in the kiss of the *alternativa,* the sponsoring bullfighter, as he invests his protégé with the right to fight the animal as a full-fledged torero for the first time. The kiss has a ritual significance originating in the idea of the exchange of the soul's breath between two persons, and like the formal salutation has a religious relationship. The sun, another one of the elements in the fiesta which is most reminiscent of its mythic origins, is inseparable from the corrida. (So much so, that no nocturnal corrida has ever proven successful. Nor is a corrida conceivable in the winter.) The torero's hat in its present form, just as in its ancient and baroque form represented in old plates of the bullfight, seems to suggest that its two points are similar to the two-pronged horns of the animal, as if a species of mysterious and sympathetic similarity existed between the fighter and his enemy. (And do not the masks and headdress of sorcerers and necromancers imitate the very spirits they want to banish?) The *traje de luces,* the suit of lights, indicates—as in any instance of singular or extravagant dress, even where it is accepted with perfect naturalness—that the dress is designed for a ritual or extraordinary function. Ritual will not allow dress that is not exceptional and rich to be used for the officiating role. Contrary to general opinion, the clothing worn by the bullfighter is not chosen primarily for ease of movement, or aptitude of any kind, nor comfort, and certainly not for defensive purposes. And the cutting of the queue: does not this, too, savor of ritual? Fairy tales and legends, closely related to myths, are filled with heroes in whose hair lies the secret of their strength.

The torero, especially the torero of other days—writes the critic Corrochano—resembled a priest: he was in his role at all times. And he possessed the manners belonging to his role; from his way of walking to his way of dressing, from his appearance to his mode of thought and feeling; the glory and elegance of his calling was symbolically present in everything he did. A glance at the image of one of the old toreros is enough to convince us of the fact that these beings polarized attention upon themselves for a reason which was "very profound," as it used to be said. Rarely did they return, at the end of the corrida, to being "private citizens."

Something of the same nature is true of the bulls as well. The populace does not want prefabricated animals. They want the "totem" of Iberia, the wild bull, the old symbol, without substitution, and they want no part of the farce of driven, lean animals. They want the corrida to be somber, hard, marked by the ancient stamp of beauty, and animated with the force of bulls which do not relent. The "shaven horns" controversy of recent years has aroused a storm of opposition to this deceit, and many a famous writer has taken arms against it.

The minority is suspicious, apt, self-sufficient, impassioned, and, very often, inopportune. It feels itself the repository of all truth and faith in the corrida, the heir to the most intransigent participants, the audience of the past, and endowed with an inquisitorial mission.

Some effort has been expended to prove that the headgear, the *traje de luces,* the queue of hair are all recent creations; even if this is proved, it is nevertheless always a point of surprise to note the ease and naturalness with which these attributes are accepted in the fiesta. There are other phenomena worthy of note: the taurine chapels with their bulls-heads; the manner of throwing the headgear to the ground, as the head of a beheaded animal (or human) might be thrown; the national mourning following the death of a celebrated torero; the sidereal encircling of the ring by the successful torero; the relics, amulets, and superstitions of those who consider death to be the denominator of life; the vast fund of occult, earthly force, that allusive force which shines forth in the richness of metaphor characteristic of "Elegy for the Death of Sánchez Mejías," of García Lorca, or in the poetry of Claudel, with his "death to Christ and life to the bull" in his ode to the Spanish martyrs. Nothing reflects the deep-seated immediacy and popular feeling for the fiesta as well as the phraseology and mannerisms which have sprung from the corrida and have enriched the common speech. The character of these phrases have proven so graphic and serviceable that in practice their figurative usage has clarified ideas that more academic language could not. The color and forcefulness of this linguistic phenomenon has led the German philologists Kolb and Hanis to write an interesting thesis concerning the influence of the corrida on Spanish periphrastic language.

And the corrida is a source of even more rewarding matter.

Christianity and the Running of the Bulls

TO EXPLAIN the deep-rooted nature and the continuity over so long a period of the Spanish national fiesta there is no better medium than a discussion of the attitude of Spanish popular Christianity to this celebration.

There is no question of "Let the capes and the bull make peace," as the great writer Quevedo would have it. Quite the opposite. Even the *villancicos,* the popular church songs, give an idea of how this fiesta was made a part of Christianity.

> Because the Queen has given birth,
> the bulls are run and tourneys sung. . . .
> kettle drums pound and clarions sound
> while seraphim fence with staffs;
> the fighters go round,
> beautifully run and gracefully pass. . . .

For thou, my Lady,
silverplate face,
I'll run my horse in this race
at a trapala, trapala, trapala pace.

And there are sermons and homilies of the same order. Fray Hernando de Santiago, in his reflections on the Gospel, speaks of the wild, mad, furious, cruel bulls: the Magnentiuses, Diocletians, Neroes, and Domitians, which in the times of those emperors, and of the martyrs, filled the amphitheatres of the empire. When Fray Antonio of Ciudad Real in 1570 spoke of the bulls, "which do honor and glory to God," and when the *villancicos* of Valdivieso told of "bringing to the ring the bull of Bethlehem," even the pious old women listening must have felt a thrill of devout awe.

The capitals of columns in the cathedral and the church of St. Saturnine, develop taurine themes, as do those in the church of Bareyo, in Santander; and the capitals in the cloister of St. Mary of the Snows, the patience worked into the choir stalls of the cathedral of Plasencia: they all speak of the bulls, just as do the popular pious books, the "*taurorum agitatio utrum licita*" of the Spanish scholastics of the Golden Age. And in the latter case, the heavy seriousness of scholastic Latin, dry and unfleshed, the gravity of the grave friars, never proved an obstacle to the light-heartedness, the street levity of the fiesta. On the balustrades of the University of Salamanca, in a plateresque language somewhat flavored with Gothicism, gentlemen jousters are shown tilting their lances at the bulls of Salamanca, drawn to enormous scale and with terrible horn tips.

In antique Spain, there was not a canonization, a transfer of the Blessed Sacrament, the first Mass of a new priest, or even a procession in a minor or major rite, without the celebration of a corrida to accompany it. The canonization of St. Theresa cost the lives of more than two hundred bulls; every convent founded by her gave its own corrida. After the canonization of St. Ignatius, the Jesuits petitioned in the chapter at Seville cathedral that a bullfight be celebrated immediately following the ceremonies. At Cáceres, those who fought the bull from horseback were automatically honorary members of the Confraternity of the Virgin. But it is superfluous to enumerate all the examples in the width and breadth of Spain.[14]

The relation between Christianity and the bulls is much more deep-seated even than appears from any cumulative enumeration of the writings of friars, of Masses said so that the bulls should fight well, or the question of whether the dean of the cathedral of Burgos wrote a treatise on tauromaquia, or whether the Navar-

[14] For bibliography on this theme see José María de Cossío, *Los Toros,* 3 vols. (Madrid, 1945) and *Los toros ante la Iglesia,* of Father Pereda.

rese theologians at Salamanca were good toreros; though all this would in itself provide endless and interesting material. But it is the very quintessence of the corrida which Christianity has assimilated, transforming and accrediting it. Something more is involved than the juxtaposition of an amusement with religion; or even of the eternal sacred character of the bull, which is less than what is suggested by Montherlant when he cites Renan to the effect that: *"que si le christianisme eût été arreté par quelle maladie mortelle, le monde eût été mithriaste."* Nor are we dealing simply with a happy marriage between the Church and the survivals of the tauromaquia. In any case, the attempt to base the true value of dogma on its vital value is profoundly anti-Catholic. The Church has always looked with the greatest suspicion on any moralizing concept of dogmatic truth. The prime distinguishing characteristic of the Church, as Romano Guardini has so well expressed it, lies in the primacy of Logos over Ethos. It is the minor truths then, simply, which palpitate at the heart of the myth, whose soul is *naturaliter cristiana,* and these truths were assimilated through sympathy and the very vitality of a people as profoundly Christian as the Spanish. And this assimilation set well, something which rarely occurs. What happened among the Spanish as regards the myth of the bull amounted to a less conventional and more spontaneous conversion of myth than the one which took place when the Renaissance converted the roses of Venus into the roses of Mary. Still, it is best not to force the simile. For what is truly Christian has to do with Christ; and in Christianity there is no doctrine, no fundamental structure of ethical values, no religious attitude, and no vital order which can be separated from the person of Christ. The attitude of the Christian populace of Spain to the corrida is analogous to the attitude of the Middle Ages in reading the classics: the classics were not read in the modern manner; rather than a historic truth, the readers sought and recognized a symbolic one; they possesed no critical or philosophic norms of interpretation; they employed instead the medieval method of allegoric and spiritual interpretation, and with it they discovered the *sensus moralis,* the *sensus antagonicus,* the *sensus mysticus* in everything they read, so that they astonish us even today by their profound unity and homogeneity, qualities which the modern world is so far from possessing in any like degree. A phenomenon unconsciously similar, then, is the Spanish reading of that ancient and ironbound text which is the corrida.

Pico della Mirandola, one of the outstanding thinkers of the Renaissance, said: *"Nulla scientia quae nos magis certificat de divinitate Christi quam Magia et Cabala."* The truth is that for the Christian thinker there exists a cosmic Christ by which everything is created, through whom everything was created. In this Christ there exists also a cosmic sympathy, and, as a character in Dostoievsky puts it, "even the animals have Christ."

In the Christian view, man has within him an angel and a beast, a horseman-knight and a horse, a *torero* and a *toro*. Man triumphs over himself when the man-angel triumphs over the man-beast, the bull with the seven terrible sharpened horns of the seven concupiscences. And all men must give battle, and all must come to the final hour of truth, the hour to make the kill. The bull must be prepared so he does not reach the final stage in his full pride and prowess. The passions must be fought with the lance, made vertiginous with the cape, weakened with the banderillas, and dispatched with brilliant incision. Our Bull, who art in our heart. And there are other battles:

> Against my five senses,
> come your five little black bulls:
> little black bull, your eyes;
> little black bull, your hair;
> little black bull, your mouth;
> little black bull, your kiss;
> and the blackest of the five,
> your body, little black bull.
>
> (*Tus cinco toritos negros*
> M. Benítez Carrasco.)

And from such an enemy those who flee plead only: Let him not toss his horns! The *pasodoble* of the fiesta is in this triumph converted to celestial music. "We serve as a spectacle to the world, to the angels and to all men," said St. Paul. And this spectacle is a highly rational one, which could not inadvertently escape the attention of Christianity. As Unamuno wrote:

> Blood runs for martyrdom
> of blackamoor or bull
> —joined in their doom—
> and the chorus full
> echoes the vaunt
> Spain! Spain is triumphant!

For Unamuno saw in the psychological battle of Prudencio, the Spanish poet who sang to the martyrs, a divine tauromaquia. The ballad of the seven capital sins, of Pemán, very well expresses this Christian vision of the bulls:

> Evening of the drover
> of the seven black bulls.
>
> Where are you going drover?
> I'm taking them into your heart.
>
> A brave corrida, that
> afternoon of my torment.
>
> Alone with a loop of silk
> mulberry silk between us.
> I, with my sword and my doubt
> against my seven desires.

So great has been the union between popular Christianity in Spain and the corrida that now the mythic element lives only in the depths of the fiesta, while on the surface above shine the resplendent Christian motes, the scintillating facets of the conqueror and mocker of death, the free play of the individual personality who moves with a liberated consciousness, the note of grace, of gentility, of spiritual elegance, of dominion over the natural world, of man as the king of creation, the primacy of the idea of liberty over the idea of destiny, the idea of confronting all phenomena directly and freely; all this in a world made more feasible, more mature, finer, and more elevated than in the ancient myths—an attitude which reminds us of the ingenuousness which Kierkegaard, the Christian Kierkegaard, detected in the very soul of the classic Hellenic world.

Our independence in the face of nature would not have been developed as it has if Christianity had not first freed us from the fascination which nature exercised over us, and by freeing us made us independent. This independence, based on the idea of God's sovereignty over the world, makes possible a certain comprehension of the world, an approach to it, a relative dominion over it which otherwise would not have been possible. There is nothing more false than the affirmation that the modern dominion over the world by means of knowledge and technology has been achieved in battle against Christianity, which would presumably have liked to keep mankind in a state of passive subjection: while the truth is that the modern development has been possible due to man's sense of personal independence dating from the time of Christ. If the nations of the East now find themselves in a backward position vis à vis the West, the explanation lies in their not having adopted Christianity, a religion which afforded man a spiritual victory over death. Father Mariana speaks of how condemned men anciently were forced to fight against wild beasts in the hunts: in the Spanish historical variant of these games no one is condemned to fight the beasts, even were they condemned to death, or were they slaves; all toreros, adds the Jesuit priest, enter the arena of their own free will.

In the end, as Eugenio d'Ors used to say, the bullfight is more than statuesque plasticity, for it is an extended, a drawn-out triumph over waylaying death, a triumph built out of a constant challenge and mockery of death. And the torero, as one great *aficionado,* Ernest Hemingway, has said, lives life with more intensity than any other man. "The art of the bullfight," he says, "is the only one in which the artist is in danger of death and in which the quality of the work of art depends on the honor of the artist." The myth, lying always in the background, has fortuitously enriched itself with new elements, magnificent hints of that Christian Greece of which Angel Ganivet, Menéndez Pelayo, and the German Romantics sometimes spoke.

The Theme of Myth in Picasso

A PROFOUNDLY new view of the corrida appears in the very first years of Picasso's work: *Course de taureaux,* 1901, when its author was twenty years old. A plaza with colors, the sun, flags, blood: elements which might have appeared in the compositions of any painter of the epoch, but here is the extraordinary capacity for strong feeling which already distinguishes the art of Picasso. A radical contrast divides the composition in two halves, one clear and the other dark, sun and shade, which at first sight suggests two distinct categories as well as two distinct seating prerogatives.[15] For in this division Picasso intimates another reality: in its essence there are two parts of the corrida; one: dark, savage, wild, formless, incarnate in the bull—"a tempest of blood and veins"; the other:

[15] In the bullfight there are two general types of tickets available, *sol* (sun) and *sombra* (shade), and thus spectators in the sun, and spectators in the shade.

clear, graceful, light-filled, distinguished by form, gesture, disdain, domination, and embodied in the torero, and also in the combination of horse and picador. This contrast lies at the basis of every corrida; it is a point which Picasso will not abandon henceforth in successive compositions.

Almost a half-century later, in 1949, a ceramic composition of his will have the same theme; the abstraction is greater, but the arena is divided in two halves: chiaroscuro, *sol-sombra*; the first, for the horse and picador, the second, for the bull. All the other elements of the plaza and its public are renounced in favor of the two halves which are decisively and distinctly traced. It is not pointlessly that the sun traverses the plaza—the zodiacal progress of Taurus is the best calculated astronomic observation in all of Spain. And in Picasso, too, it is not haphazard. We will see the same preoccupation in other paintings of his; it is central to his work, a bit of marrow; serious, profoundly tragic; and, amidst all his affectation of the shocking and disconcerting, it does not leave his work.

In the two paintings, *Mise à mort,* 1934, and *Course de taureaux,* 1923, Picasso shows us, alone in the arena, a horse and a bull. The two are shown at the moment of death; one is as much an animal as the other. And yet, they each wear totally different expressions. For Picasso always insists, throughout his work, on the same general horse and the same general bull: in the horses,

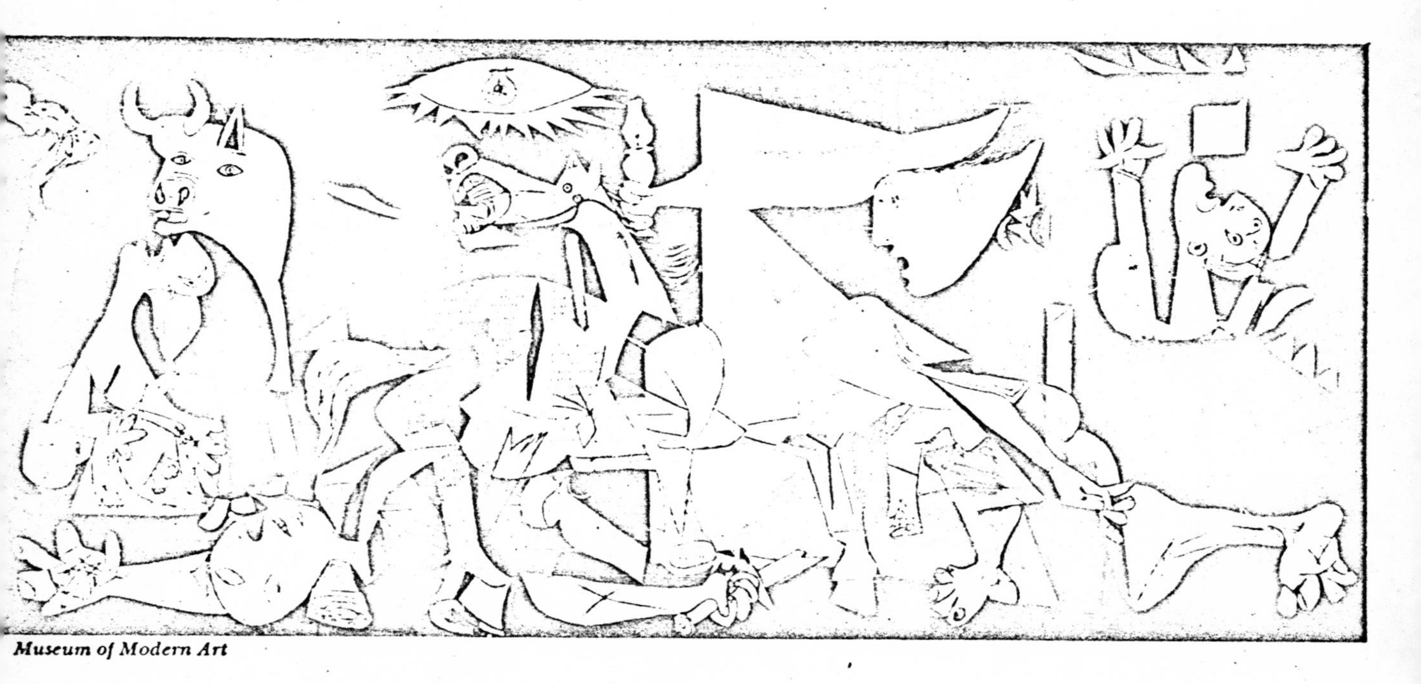

Museum of Modern Art

GUERNICA

Courtesy of the Art Institute of Chicago

THE WOUNDED PICADOR

shown without bridles or saddles, there is never anything repellent or horrible. They are neither stylized nor are they lacking in forcefulness. There is something indomitable about them, but there is also something innocent, a kind of purity, the calmness of the horse which has nobly ridden between the perils of life and the spur. White is the preferred color for these horses. And they have been endlessly repeated as a theme.

As a marginal comment it is worthwhile citing Chesterton's comment that the noblest figure cut amidst humanity is that formed by a man on a horse, a symbol of nobility, and, as the Spanish wording succinctly puts it, appropriately enough, a *caballero a caballo,* for the origin of cavalier is in the word for horse. Where in the past the horse has not appeared, civilization has not appeared either. And wherever the spirit has triumphed over matter, there the horse has been a natural ally. The horse has shown man the value of force without cruelty. The horse is valiant, and yet does not know what it means to be fierce. The victories with which it has to do are those which leave the heart complacent. It was from the horse that the Greeks learned the secret of a force which unfolds with grace. A Latin-American thinker, the Mexican Vasconcelos, inspired by the feats of the horses of the Spanish Conquistadores in his own country, has written a magnificent eulogy to the horse. He points out how the horse ennobles the habits of a people, and how it influences their garb and their dance, their gallantry and their dealings with each other. One need only to recall the fifteen horses of Hernán Cortés, handsomely described by Bernal Díaz against the calm and joyful horizon of New Spain. And in the bull, too, there is majesty, haughtiness, lordly expressiveness. The image of a bull on the range, in the fields, quiet, tranquil, moving its head as it follows with fixed gaze the steps of the passer-by, is a powerful one. The bull is lord of the green pastures, a worthy beast, and to its inborn power it unites the quality which keeps it from submitting to fear even when it is deceived. It does not attack with the object of devouring, as do other beasts. Assured in its power, it attacks without heed to the danger, and never treacherously. The bull boasts a presence, a drive, whether in the early frolicking stage or the gravity of maturity. Its slow, majestic movement evidences its qualities of caste.

The combination, the complex formed by the bullfighter and the bull is as impressive as is the unity of horseman and horse. Popular fancy has given the name "half-moon" to the bull's horns, and calls the passes made by the torero with his cape "the dance of the colors," and, even more incisively, "the mocker mocking death." The last two phrases indicate the dominion of the man.

• Picasso accentuates the monstrous aspect in the bull, an attribute which the bull does not in truth possess in itself. He paints a bull that is almost a dragon. These bulls are not electric, agile, stylized *à la* Goya, svelte and handsome, silhouetted by a zigzag. Violating the reality of appearances, but profoundly concerned with the matter in hand, Picasso goes deeper in his exposition of an ultimate truth and reality, which, like myth, is within us all. It was not capricious of him to twist the hooves of the bull, to make the eyes appear bedevilled. A head disproportionate to the body, teeth belonging to a colossus, deformed shoulders almost joined to the hooves: this is the same art which stretches the neck of the horse, making it an innocent Pegasus, which at its death desires to fly—for of all the quadrupeds it was the first to give man the illusion of being winged. Man must not have felt himself the master of the earth until the horse gave him this first illusion.

> Horse that in thirty paces
> will die on the sand . . .
> Your soul will go flying
> while your legs are dying.
> Fly, little dead horse!
> The soul has no reins,
> and the winds no whips
> nor the angels spurs.
>
> (*Toros en Sevilla,* A. del Valle)

The bull, for its part, resists ferociously. It protests and persists in its protest. Picasso proposes that we look at the *plus ultra,* at the inner essence of everything with our sight alone. That we look only with our sight, and with it judge what we see and what surrounds us. And yet his art has never been content with appearances. For he is a painter who has never sinned as a materialist or a naturalist, a sin into which so many other painters have fallen frequently and unconsciously.

In Picasso's art, the same facility serves him to humanize the beasts as to brutalize the men. The old saying fits here like a ring to the finger: *anima quodamodo omniam.* In an art like his, a universality of expression is made possible and comes to be understood eventually, despite the incomprehension of many as regards the technical aspects of his work, marvelous as these are. The *Face of a Bull,* dated May 21, 1931, is more than a bull, and yet, underneath it all, it is a bull too. The image is known to everyone, for it lives urbanely among us: it is the face of brutality itself. The lower part of the face is the most pronounced in the drawing: full cheeks; thick, tight lips; the nostril dilated. The upper part of the drawing is devoid of any nobility, the forehead is narrow, the gaze fixed. It is a beast and yet something more.

The *Head of a Horse,* May 2, 1937, painted on cloth, symbolizes Picasso's horse: terror-stricken, defeated, pursued, the victim which one more time carries within it the cold, strong blade of the lance that wounds all of its life.

This manner of presenting bulls and horses, the very frequency of the presentation, is not an exclusive creation, something original with Picasso. It would be easy to think so, but the elements involved relate, even more than to the myth in its ancient or classic form directly to the Spanish people itself, to its live and popular argot. The Spaniard, when he refers to the bull, in addition to giving it an active role, makes it the agent of danger, the author of a stroke of bad fortune. *Le cogió el toro* (the bull caught—and tossed—him) , *que te pilla el toro* (the bull will get you) , *ciertos son los toros* (sure and certain are the bulls) , *echarle a uno el toro* (to set the bull on some one) , *tener más intención que un toro* (to be more designing than a bull) , *hecho un toro* (to turn into a bull) , *tirarse al ruedo* (throw oneself into the ring) , *ver los toros desde la barrera* (see the bulls from the ringside) , *lidiar contra el destino* (to engage fate as if it were the bull), *los toros dan las cornadas y Dios se encarga de repartirlas* (the bulls make the horn thrusts and God takes responsibility for their distribution). . . . The image of the threatening bull fills Spanish everyday language with figures of speech, and from argot has passed into art: in metaphor, symbol, allegory.

In the mind of the Spaniard, the horse, along with the dog, is an animal which believes, *a priori,* in the indisputable superiority of man. The relationship between the two has made the horse more intelligent and less bestial. As Quevedo says:

What a sight it is to see
a Spanish grandee
short-stirupped in the saddle
expending a horse in a tourney!

The horse is also an object of fond affection, saviour on the old high-roads, the faithful friend in the gypsy camps, the sympathetic accomplice in the robber band, the highwayman's helper. A common saying in Spain runs to the effect that when you are convinced your horse is a brute, you should dismount, and, before remounting, take a hundred riding lessons. What is the mystery of these heavy unfeathered flyers? From them sprang the marvelous race of the centaurs; then, too, Pegasus, a creature of curious locomotion, heavier than air.

When the bull is thought of in all its brute force, wild and dark, and the horse is remembered as being something light, more elevated, more *ours*, closer to us, even angelic and winged, we are not far from the popular imagination, nor from the mythical either. The really surprising (and characteristic) fact about Picasso's view of all this is that in his work the bull almost always triumphs over all else. And this is the key to the taurine vision of Picasso. The horse does not exist, nor the bullfighter either, who can resist *his* bulls, nor is there any kind of bullfighting which will serve. His bulls, quintessentially *the* bull, are lords of the world which he paints. And what we feel, what we are all certain of, is that the bull in Picasso signifies something more than a problem of form *qua* artistic and pure form. Even if his art, like any great art, has no point, it is always possessed of a sense, a sense which never speaks as clearly from his canvasses as when he paints the bull, whatever his style of painting it.

In the struggle between the bull and the horse, as in *Course de taureaux*, 1934, two curves are counterposed one to another, as if two totally opposed systems met head on, as if two tense, vibrant arcs clashed: the light curve of the horse and the dark curve of the bull, both locked within the confines of the *ruedo*, the taurine arena, whose limits seem to press upon the two figures, as if there were no human beings in the *plaza de toros*. The bull, his head compressed, small, disproportionate, does not attack with his horns alone; rather he attempts to bite the horse under the saddle, precisely where the horse is best protected. More than a vision, the painting appears constructed mentally; still, basically it encompasses a vision of reality. The head of the bull is finally transformed into a species of iron pincers, an instrument with black entrails. The horse, always the victim, desperately stretches his neck and extends his legs. Spectators startled from their seats are projected close up, into the orbit of the beast. For Picasso the arena is like the communal well, at whose rim the entire village gathers.

The dominion of the bull, its imperiousness, is the theme which is most often repeated in his work. The sword nailed in the animal's nape in *Course de taureaux,* September 1933, does not prevent it from being so powerful that it carries the horse and the bullfighter himself along on its back. And then he paints toreros with the breasts of women showing beneath their costumes, where he has exposed them and discovered their debility. There is very little brilliant footwork for the torero to perform before the bulls Picasso paints. There is little in his canvases of the fatal whirlpool of horse, bull and picador. In his vision the bull lords it over all other contenders.

In another picture, *Minotauromaquie,* 1935, there is only decision, tenacity, force in the monstrousness of the bull. The rest is flight, innocence, pain. The horse is subjugated before the beast; the bullfighter is a woman; a girl who appears to have no notion of what is involved carries a branch of flowers, a light—as if another act of homage were involved, one which would be the refutation of all public homages. Two women appear seated on a stone piazza; an older man, bearded, flees in nakedness; the sword is drawn in such a way that it is not clear whether the torero is intent on suicide or the bull is holding it. The beast is completely dominant, threatening, decisive, a mixture of brutality and repulsiveness, a minotauromaquia emerging from the sea, eternal symbol of the inexhaustible, pouring into the plaza, into the privacy of the home, into all public spectacles and homages, into all gestures of tenderness. . . .

From the year 1934 alone there are more than a dozen works in which Picasso repeats, intensely and always new, his view not only of the bulls but also of his time. Often the horse lifts its hands, a species of wings, before the charge of the furious bull attacking without pity. At other times the bull leaps upon the horse in order to bite it, or the horse is impaled on the horns of the beast. The horses' necks stretch as if to escape the material world. Horses and bulls together, against the dark background of the one, the light-filled silhouettes of the other, one always counterposed to the other. For instance, in the drawing of Boisdeloup, April 13, 1935, the horse is possessed with fear, in desperation pressing its head to its chest, its hooves sunken in the sand, its eyes starting from their sockets, while the bull licks itself with relish. And, even when he is dwelling upon themes which appear vulgar, Picasso goes far deeper than his immediate subject matter.

A goodly part of the engravings of Picasso are given over to representation of bulls and horses: the bull and the horse, of 1927, to illustrate a work of Balzac; the fallen picador and the pic-work of 1929; the etchings, and engravings on zinc, of 1921, are filled with the same tragic duality. In one of the 1921 zinc engravings the horse claws his way up and raises his head in a dramatic invocation; a heavy, short-horned bull charges him venomously. In these engravings, filled with a heavy, tragic spirit of obscurity, Picasso makes use of exquisite figure interpretations, defined only in contour, with a simplicity and purity which brings this work close to that of the Greek vase.

These works of Picasso, where bulls and horses appear singly in their simple and luminous individuality, can serve as a basis for the comprehension of the drawings of 1937. More than illustrative, they are also visionary. These bulls and horses never quite die. They are there, always entire, in the midst of a rending tension, while neither one nor the other achieves final triumph. What is their significance? The artist tells us only that one is the side of the bull and the other that of the horse; between them a furious rivalry, an inhuman, bloody, and one-sided battle between the animals in a corrida.

There are many other works which we could cite in relation to this aspect of his art. The studies made in connection with *Guernica,* ceramics, lithographs, illustrations in the most diverse styles and forms of which the most remarkable are the engravings for an edition of the *Tauromaquia de Pepe-Hilo,* planned by the publisher Gustavo Gili, with a preface by Montherlant. (Some of these pieces can be seen in the book Geiser made of Picasso's engravings.)[16]

[16] More recently, in the two large volumes called *Picasso Lithographie,* with notes and a catalogue by Fernand Mourlot, this vision of the corrida reappears, as in "La Gran Corrida," Vol. II, p. 183 (1947-49), dated March 11, 21, 31, 1949; the image of the monstrous bull, appears in Vol. I, pp. 78, 79.

Though in some of his paintings Picasso has introduced animals which recall paper birds, or picadors with the air of dragon-flies, horses resembling insects and toreros who appear to save themselves from the rays of the sun by standing under parasols, as well as bulls which are too formidable in their horribleness, still, there is that in his work which is not caprice, not preciousness, but altogether the contrary.

In the bulls of Picasso there is no arbitrariness, nor pure forms which do not answer to a concrete content. To go to the bulls with Picasso, to accompany him to the bullring is to be sure of witnessing always "a bad afternoon." And not a bad afternoon in the bullring of a ranch at the edge of some lost village in Spain, or in the *plaza de toros* of any Latin-American capital; but, rather, to witness the bad afternoon of the West itself. Without falling back on allegory, or symbols, Picasso has seen, as has no one else, the concrete reality in the corrida, and has seen it with such force and penetration that, in touching its very depths, its ultimate meaning, he has given the power of speech to the universal element. This is the prodigy of his projection from the blooded Spanish ingredient to the transcendental and ecumenical. He does not strive to create something new, but to plumb what is given, what is made flesh and blood in the most popular form. His painting, as he has said, does not search, but finds.

In the corrida Picasso accentuates the element of contrast, the bi-polarity; the oppositions, the chiaroscuro, the bull/horse. He provides no way out, there are no exits. We find ourselves in the alleyway of a gnostic ringside of bi-polarities. He does not exhaust the ultimate phases of the bullfight, but remains in the world of the animal. The torero is minimized, he scarcely appears.

In some of the representations of horses and bulls, especially in his drawings—where he tends to introduce the abstract form, so that the spectator can forego all commentary—the oviform sign comes to mind at once, the continuous circle known to orientalists, and to investigators of Aryan civilization, and known too, and most significantly, in the ornamentation of the Basques, from which race, let us state it at once, Picasso descends on his father's side.

This kind of circle is obtained by describing a circumference and then drawing a diameter, followed by a semi-circle on each radius, on one side and the other of the original diameter. If the latter line is then erased, the figure remaining is the only medium for dividing the circumference of the circle in two equal parts, complementary and congruent. In the minds of the primitive men who first constructed this figure, the halves symbolized the opposed principles of life, light and dark,

good and evil, male and female: dualisms, all of them, familiar to oriental concepts of life, and profoundly combatted by trinitarian Christianity when they appeared in Gnosticism in the first centuries of our era.

There are drawings of Picasso in which we clearly get the impression that they were built out of this oviform and under its sign. Representations of mother and child are frequent in all epochs of his painting, especially in the final drawings of 1937, where the continuous, biologic, incessant movement of life seems to enclose itself within the two halves of an oviform. In his drawings of bulls and horses (in *A Pablo Picasso,* by Paul Eluard) there are times when the two congruent halves emanate from the background. But in the end the duality is completely resolved, and the circle is broken: the bull will dominate, nothing will serve as balance against it.

The torero, the central figure of the corrida, is minimized, he scarcely appears; in a worthy manner, never. He is always hemmed in by the bull, or he is in full flight. This is the obsession in Picasso's tauromaquia. And the fact that the torero does not occupy in Picasso's art a position corresponding in any way with his importance and key function in the corrida is not because the artist does not need him in the composition of the group, but because Picasso's torero occupies a special role—one outside the limits of his art.

Breeches of gold velveteen
sash dark green, the jacket
laced with silk, and orange
the hue of the socks.
On patent-leather shoes
the double butterflies are silverplate.

(*A Pepe Hillo,* Villalon)

Nowhere in this art appear the melancholic toreros with knit brows, the hard, dark look, the jaw set, short and strong muscled, encircling the bull, unfurling the cloth, rising to the heavens of tauromaquia. Nothing in these pictures vibrates in the torero's art as it is supposed to, "like the breeze in the marsh reeds." There is no suggestion here of light, blood, gold, sun, of visible and natural angel going from one side to the other. Dressed in light, in gold and scarlet, the torero is thrust into the world above the shoulders of the mob

now resounding and sounding
the hollow clap and echoing band,
and of a sudden the flare
of a young god trodding the sand.

before him, the godling
naked, unarmed, alone: a bull.

(*Oda a Belmonte,* Gerardo Diego)

But Picasso determines to dwell only on the institution of the horns

for the bull of heaven shall
fell the horses of the sun.

(Góngora)

• Picasso keeps the bull from total triumph, he keeps fate at bay, he credits it, as Don Juan does death. In his art there is no redemption; the action takes place amid struggle, upheaval, as anguished as it is desperate; and yet the bull is nowwhere glorified, which would be an absurdity.

• But, the bull—this dark mass of blood and earth who refuses to submit to any of the forms of subjugation proposed by the torero—is the central figure in Picasso's work; and this bull appears to have no special moral significance, nor any determined symbolism, but is simply a plastic representation of the projection of brutality upon a world grown more than ever passive.

I know. The hours will return
with their head of a black
bull, suddenly appearing, brutal,
on the road without turn.

(*Cara a cara,* Guillén)

"With you is the night imprisoned,"
delimited, inert;
with you is the night become as a bond.

(*Chiquero,* Rafael Morales)

... last night your owner dreamt
black bull, a dream
black bull, of blood:
death in each horn,
and pain in each stream
of tortured blood.

(*La toríada 831,* Villalón)

The night, a black bull, is departing,
—flesh of full mourning, and of fright, and of
mystery—
which bellowed, immensely and terrible,
above the sweating fear of the fallen;
and the day comes up a fresh child.

The black bull emerges alone, meet and handsome,
over the cold green dawn, upon a blue peak.
He lows south to north, repudiating
the deep blue zenith, still starry
with the great stars
stuck on his endless horns.

(*Aurora de Moguer, Desvelo,* Juan Ramón Jiménez)

bad person of a bull

(Rafael Alberti)

But, after all, what is the significance of the bull in Picasso? It is a vision, so that the artist does not limit himself to saying I have seen it this way, or that, or I was moved or illuminated. The vision itself determines the manner and mode of what happens.

As in the Homeric mimesis, and the great visions of Dante, the truth does not rest merely in an acute observation of daily happenings, but also in an *a priori* representation of destiny. That is, a mere copy of phenomena will not suffice. The representation must not simply evolve out of observation, but from the depths of the myth. And there is a unity of content in the representation which is given, which is prior to the observation.

None of this is to say that observation, truthfulness, naturalness are not part of the representation. But first comes the vision and the mimesis, the mimicry. Kierkegaard discovered, as Socrates before him, that the best method of communicating with men was by indirection. Like Kierkegaard and Socrates, Picasso does not present us with ready-made truths. He helps men illumine the truth by their own means. Picasso lies within the sphere of myth, of mystery, and not the sphere of utopia, nor even the sphere of the problem, especially when he paints bulls. He has shown a definite preference for myth, which evolves in his consciousness through action, rather than for utopia, or the description of a future state—a method which is like taking minute notation of a dream in the expectation of later witnessing its realization. He has preferred the vision seen at the height of action. One goes to utopia; on the other hand, one is *in* myth, one proceeds from it. Myth nourishes us as long as we hold to it, even if we do not attain what we seek.

In Picasso, myth is born, not so much from faith as from violence, even from desperation. His work is not—done in the face of a problem which must be resolved, but within a mystery which must be lived in order to be understood. Problem is that which we find in its entirety before us; mystery, on the other hand, involves us, compromises us; and it is not before us, it surrounds us. And it is only from this point of view that the roots of Picasso's art can be understood. Severini, after studying three hundred Picasso paintings in various exhibitions, permits himself (in his *Treatise on the Plastic Arts)* to conclude that Picasso does not belong so much to the "pictorial" as to the sphere of "action"; this, despite the undoubted pictorial value of Picasso's work, which Severini believes, however, is secondary to the great artist's importance as an *impulsive* force in art, that is, a revolutionary, renovating force, tending toward absolute liberty, a will to freedom more decisive than his realized work, his pictorial accomplishment.

Picasso's "action" is an accomplishment of a different order, and one destined to clarify painting, to nourish it in a hundred different ways. For this painter's influence is more intellectual and moral than it is purely pictoric. Picasso is an exception in the history of painting; his function is not that of other painters; it is not only a matter of art with him but also an attitude toward existence; to judge his work, aestheticism is not enough; moreover, in addition to the aesthetic mystery in his work, there is the human one, though in our study it must be viewed through the intermediacy of animals, through the cult of the animal. This cult of the animal, be it said, is of wide diffusion in the history of humanity, so much so that there are scholars who consider it more natural to humanity than the worship of gods with human form; even when men began to represent gods with their own human visage the cult of the animal remained tenaciously alive. For instance, in Egypt the cult persisted to the end of the ancient culture. Whenever a god has first appeared in animal form, he resists ever abandoning this form entirely, and his human body may be completed by an animal head. If today we feel once again the eloquence of the animal spirit in art, may we not consider it a matter of human regression? All this surprises us today because man has assumed supreme dignity in our eyes. We characterize him by his intelligence, and we know that there is no superiority beyond the reach of intelligence, nor inferiority for which it will fail to compensate. It was not thus, Bergson explains, when intelligence had not yet proven itself.[17] The intervention of intelligence in most matters was

[17] Bergson, *Les Deux Sources de la Morale et de la Religion*, 1932.

still too limited to reveal its infinite power to invent; the arms and tools adopted by man did not stand favorable comparison to the equipment native to animals. Even man's ability to reflect, which is the secret of his power, at that time produced an impression of debility, inasmuch as it is a quality leading to indecision, while the animal's reaction, truly instinctive, is immediate and certain. And then, the silence of the animal might seem like disdain—as if it had something better to do than engage us in conversation. All this might explain why humanity has shown no aversion toward the cult of the animal. And yet, how explain in our own century the eighth of the *Duineser Elegie,* of Rilke, or the role of the bull in the art of Picasso, or even the role of the eagle, the swan, the pigeon in poetry, in literature in general? It must be noted that in the cult of the animal, the animal is worshipped because of some characteristic property. The nature of the animal seems to be concentrated in a unique quality; it is clear that its individuality is dissolved in the generic: to recognize a man consists in distinguishing him from other men, but to recognize an animal, generally, is to recognize what species it belongs to; an animal, even if perfectly concrete and individual, is considered for its special quality and considered in its genus. And it is the genera which pass into language and myth. But the language of men has not only become simpler and more rudimentary than ever, but also violent. The intercession of the human spirit is constant, and infinite its modes of invention, but no less manifest is its impotence to achieve any deep understanding in a culture disintegrating as never before. The arms and tools of which man/angel avails himself do not stand up to those devised by man/animal; moreover, the equipment of the man/animal is found in a superior state among the animals, where activity is simple, of a single piece, oriented in one direction. And in the work of Picasso this direction is represented by the way of the bull, and all he implies. For this reason we were saying before that myths change from one place to another, suffer contagion from one or another impurity, change their primitive character in one way or another, but all the while preserve a continuity in their inner essence. Picasso, child of the century, in painting terrible, repellent bulls expresses a truth regarding the period of history in which we all must live. His protest and revolt are the protest and revolt of the artist. A moralist, a preacher, a philosopher, a politician, would have made it in another way.

In order to emphasize the role of the bull, Picasso exploits and also exaggerates his battle with the horse. Of all the participants in the corrida the horse is the most innocent, the most defenseless, the object of everyone's pity: ancient and hopeless jades, they appear in the plaza blindfolded. In these horses Picasso has found the polar opposite to the bull; just as the innocent, the defenseless, are counterposed to the brave, to brute force and the crushingly triumphant. It matters not that the work with the pic has no longer any pivotal importance, any more importance in the corrida than the work with the cape, the muleta, or the banderillas! Picasso has more than enough reasons to accentuate the impotence of the horse, and to make the bull synonymous with cruelty, brutality, with the dark shodaw lying across the face of time, the *mal-de-siècle,* century-sickness, the profound ill which he has proposed to paint. Still, Picasso does not float on clouds of mythological disquisition. Any reader can find, in any one of the dozens of books on Picasso, infinite anecdotes to confirm the fact that he is not carried about on clouds: the leap from the mythological to the everyday is as habitual as it is consequential in this artist, and one more proof of the vitality and expressiveness of the bull in his work.

For the first number of the surrealist journal *Minotaure,* in 1933, Picasso drew the cover, a heavy-set minotaur with broad shoulders, human, hairy, lusty, with a tail. The most surprising feature is that it is the minotaur who has the sword in its hand; no human hero is in sight.

It is not surprising to find, at the foot of another horrible monster—a mixture of bull, fish, eagle and horse, the following inscription by the painter:

4 Nov. XXXV

I watched emerge
this evening
from the concert
at the Salle Gaveau
the last
person
and then I went a little further along the
same street to the tobacco counter
to get matches.

No need to deal with all the many taurine works of Picasso, filled with a Picasso fauna of centaurs, minotaurs, and appearing in lithographs, ceramics, still-life; we will do well to concentrate on the most successful of his treatments of the bull.

In his great work *Guernica,* there are no ruins, no smashed houses or chimneys to remain standing in the rubble like giant's fingers pointing to the sky; the scanty flames in the picture are as small as the crest of a rooster. Within the space, which could be an interior or could be *plein air,* there are only limbs and faces destroyed by fright and terror. The drama is an intimate one, so that only the faces betray its effects. In the midst of the humans are the horse and the bull. The horse is in the center of the canvas, its side transfixed by a lance, its mouth opened wide in a final cry, the tongue in the shape of a dagger. At its feet lies the rider, his sword broken. A figure who seems to have descended from heaven through a door suddenly thrust open pushes a lamp ahead of him. In the triangle of light which is formed from the two lower sides of the canvas up to the central height an anguished woman directs herself up to where the light begins, and in this illuminated area the central group of sufferers is structured. On the left, outside the area of light, a threatening bull with curled tail dominates the entire composition; its snout seems to rest on the head of a desperate mother carrying the swaddling clothes of her dead child. At the other end, on the right, a man is caught in flames. All the mouths are open; the hands, where the lines of the tragedy are written, are also open. The black, white, grey, maroon tones match the emotions of the drama. An electric bulb, the sun of disillusion, furnishes the rays of the only sun to shed light on these unfortunates. But a bird is flying, perhaps one raised by the very protests of the moribund horse, and it sings its song of life. The luminous triangle, too, despite the destruction, and the disarticulation of a composition reflecting bombardments and its effects, lends unity and force to the whole, as it tenses and sustains it. The bull triumphs over the work of desolation and chaos, wherein the cry of beings sacrificed to the cruelty of the world still rings out.

From this plastic composition it might be possible to make a meaningful juxtaposition by abstracting the fundamental themes: "the triangle," "transfixed by a lance," "the bird," "the victim," "the light from on high"; a dogmatic interpretation would be far-fetched, but still, there is at least a secularized Christian influence here. We can almost think of a Crucifixion, where the cross stands between the two thieves and the light of the sky forms a luminous triangle falling from the height. Rembrandt, perhaps?

The transcendent nature of this canvas has been obscured by a dismal political propaganda. And many people have chosen to see in it a work of propaganda, especially when it was first exposed to the French public in a pavillion facing the German representation in an exposition. The fact that Picasso identified his painting with the name of a city is a result of his profoundly realistic sense, which seeks always the concrete, the historic and still alive. Whatever political element there is in the painting is absorbed in the spiritual dimension, beyond all histrionics. The canvas, today more than ever, is no longer an illustration of one specific bombardment, but the picture of all bombed cities. It is the drama of thousands of European cities, impotent before brute force, before the bull of evil, whatever the flags it flies.

Picasso seems to speak his ultimate word on the bull

in his *Skull of a Bull on a Table,* 1942. In this work, and in a surprising manner, the bull acquires his maximum expression. A deep and horrible solitude pervades the canvas. Everything is dead and fleshless; and yet, it all lives, in an inconceivable manner and with inconceivable force, even the table, which seems to serve as neck, shoulders, and over which is draped a cape, in the Spanish fashion. Everything is dark; darkness presses at the windows; the white streak, more than a crack letting in light, seems like a cry in the night. But nothing is more eloquent than the expression which lives in the articulation of the jawbones, in the conjunction of the nerves—all tenacity, grasping, bite. Everything is made clear, so that no word can be said more. There is no "other" one present here; nothing but the sense of aloneness caught in the throat, in the windpipe, a need to bite one's lips. The inferior maxillaries seem to prolong themselves into two arms which hold something in their hands, and the jaws grind and chew against themselves. The more one looks, the more one discovers. At length, it is difficult not to admire the vitality and the profound experience the painter has infused into the very marrow of the beast; at the same time one is moved frenetically to a kind of laughter at the skull of a bull exposed in like manner. No artist has ever created anything more deeply horrible, and yet the painter has remained free of the theme and above the subject. Here is the bull, the bull which all men carry within them. Beyond it is despair, so complete that it can not resist itself.

The variety and richness of expression of the bull in Picasso is limitless, for wide is the domain of the beast. Consider *The Rape of Europa,* of 1946, a post-war piece: Europa with protruberant breasts, and hands which securely and strongly grasp the horns of the bull. What the bull signifies in Picasso we can now at least conjecture; but if we compare this bull with the others, and consider the lamentable and insecure position of Europe in the post-war period, it is impossible to tell whether nostalgia is involved or if it is not rather one more sarcasm by the painter. But when all is said and done, it is the mythical figure of the bull which rapes Europe.

The shadow of Bull in the "Figures" of Picasso

IN THE WORK of Picasso, the bull is like one of those Spanish rivers, turbulent and agitated, which lose themselves among brambles, rocks, and reeds, only to reappear later at some other place further on, in plain sight. There are times when it appears that the bull is adumbrated even in the "figures" of the painter, figures as profound as they are debatable and enigmatic.

Very much a man of the 20th century, Picasso is a stupendous assimilator of all techniques, even when he appears to forego them all. As various as his figures may be his aim is always that of a sharpshooter, his phobia against the vacuum always absolute. *Épater le bourgeois,* and much more. He can always call upon the nervous hypersensibility which constituted the strength of his first productions, which led him to divorce himself from the formal and objective. He will gather strength from the store of forces which earlier pushed him to a sound and natural development; and he will make use, too, of the elements which caused him to lose force; he will take elements of his art from the pseudo-intellectual and the pseudo-scientific; from his marvelous feeling for purified tones; from the nonsense surrounding him. But his figures, despite their *simultaneism,* their radical ugliness, the hallucinatory mysticism, the stunning virtuosity of his caprice, the "checkered blushes," as Ramón Gómez de la Serna says, "enigmatic drawings which could serve as rugs in a madhouse for magnates," despite all this, his figures are not essentially fantastic, or unreal; Picasso paints a truth, a fact, a concrete phenomenon, consequently traced, wherein his characters do not even lack an intimate sense: the profound solitude which characterizes them and the deep anguish left in the world in the shadow of the bull of evil.

In the heads or tails of his art what difference does it make if the necks of some of his "figures" are made of *papier collé,* or if his bathers bathe in beaches of sandpaper! As far as art is concerned, it is a matter of indifference whether the St. Mathew Passion of Bach he played on strings made from the guts of hogs, or whether the paint used by Giotto was made of oleaginous substances or something else.

Picasso is continuously experimenting. He feels his way, and the critics waste their time discovering orphic cubisms, techtonic pathos, calligrames of surfaces—all

Courtesy of the Art Institute of Chicago

COMBAT

HEAD OF BULL

THE WOUNDED HORSE

matters and problems of form, which are often no more than the mathematics of boredom, outside the plastic ends which his work entails. The suggestions of his sensibility disdain such trigonometries, by means of which some of his emulators strive to imitate his fantasy alone. In a letter published in 1926, Picasso said: "I have always painted for my time and I don't load myself up with the facts of research. What I see, I represent oftentimes in one way and oftentimes in another." Picasso is not an "impurist," a versatile performer, a voluble artist. He is devoted to a loyalty higher than "loyalty." The celebrated Spanish critic Eugenio d'Ors himself admits it. And Picasso continues to be as much Picasso as ever, following the so-called "return to Ingres," just as the De Falla of the *Concerto* was the same as the one of *Las noches* or *El amor brujo,* and the same Stravinsky was the author of *Petrouchka* as of *Le Sacre,* after his so-called "return to Bach."

The theme of Guernica left its mark on all his later work, to such a degree that his art was totally transformed. He broke with the traditional representation of figures; he gives them a significance related to contemporary sensibility. Monstrous, it has been said. And also terribly beautiful, filled with human truth.

For instance, the *Head of a Man,* September 4, 1938: the head covered with something which is between a clown's cap and an object resembling a tricorne; a bag of skin which holds the eyes of a nobody, a mean-spirited anonymity; something like a pig's snout; hermetic, dry, vengeful, out-of-luck; the egocentric gesture of the hands across the unarrogant chest reveals the mean and miserly nature; and yet, it is not that simple. The truth is that the painting contains many souls. The expression of the mouth, pert and fresh, is different from that of the eyes. If nature and technique seem to have a single tongue, the language of the spirit has many. Despite everything, this figure, within its black world, possesses the hieratical quality of a religious miniature of the eleventh century. The constructive discipline of lines that know what they want has the effect of lending the gift of gesture to the objects surrounding the figures too. The crosspiece of the chair is confused with the meshwork of the collar.

And consider the repugnant reality of this other *Figure,* September 10, 1938: a heap of rush, with the nose of a horse, under the pastry-cook's clownish hat; again the most compelling feature are the eyes. The right eye is open in a caracol form, it widens like the circular waves of a pool: frightened, cold, calculating, like that of a fresh-water fish. The other eye, wearing a different expression, is without light, submissive, treacherous. The waves are curved, clashing and losing direction the moment they hit against each other. Two different expressions are joined within the one repellent body; there is the preceptive chair, which in Picasso is a kind of emblem of the bourgeois quality he ridicules. The figure has no hands; its mane is at the mercy of the wind. The composition as a whole is a mixture of rubbish and shreds; a repellent whole which Picasso never tires of presenting, as if he possessed the secret of the mould which turns out the true sign.

Consider also the two studies titled *Seated Woman in Armchair,* 1941, each one in her own chair; both works date from the same year, even the same month, as is made clear in the magnificent *Editions de Chêne,* where more than half the reproductions are *Portraits of Women,* in the style we are discussing. Seated in the preceptive chair, wearing a hat, is a gay *demoiselle* with the head of a talking parrot; other indicative forms point to her being empty-headed, moved by delusions, without profundity whatever, verbose, without weight, a complainer, possessed, lacking even a neck for support; her shoulders appear to droop from the back of the chair like clothes hung to dry; her attitude is aggressive, her arms raised in a gesture of aggression; the head of the eternally-surprised one turned about in the look of eternal stupidity.

The other 1941 *Seated Woman* wears a different expression. There is none of the spiritual thinness of the other; her nose belongs to the thick fauna of Picasso: she is more repellent, more mechanical in the gesture of her arms, more vulgarly dressed, her mechanistic nature underscored by the lines which cut across her middle; the eyes of a prying woman, homely as a goose; she seems to be standing, even to be walking, but the chair, her eternal burden, and the disconcerting colors, do not let her go; the chair itself is like a plexiglass coat thrown over her shoulders.

Another *Figure*, dated April 12, 1945: two different faces are revealed, on one and the same body, in the same chair; one of them, in the skeletal form of a simpleton, the other, more human, emerging from the neck of the first, more determined, stern, and hard-mouthed; the long hair of one obscures the vision of the other. In one body, reside two differently-colored souls. The hands of one serve the ends of the other; the chair itself serves as a cane. Atomizing, taking apart, unravelling the subject is one of the favorite devices of the epoch; the feeling supplied by the play of light in the work of the impressionists is today provided by the representation of simultaneous figures, superimposed, opened out, unravelled: perhaps it is not so much a technical caprice of the artist as it is a plastic phenomenon arising in unravelled societies, in cultures lacking personality.

For his "figures," Picasso does not seem to limit himself to the animal world alone in his search for resources and means of expression. He makes use also of the mechanical spirit and the soul of technology. For instance, he hangs a species of hook from the eyebrows of these figures, and they appear to open and shut their eyes mechanically.

Consider, too, his studies for the Guernica masterpiece. Beings possessed by the machine, overcome by it, show their denuded inner essence; the anatomy of mechanism is exposed. The hard look is not enough. To express this hardness better (in a *Figure* dated April 27, 1938), the artist makes use of a species of water wheels or small brass wheels fixed into the very pupils; wires, ravelled threads run in every direction; the wheels seem to spin endlessly, suggesting the interior of a factory; everything is totally hard, steel-like: the inflexible and the inhuman prevail.

A drawing dated August 10, 1938, reveals another unfortunate. A neck, which might be the axis of a handmill or of a rotating press; the uncovered face is a mechanism, all its gears showing; there is nothing noble or human in it; only pieces of machinery; screws. In order to discover the true visage it would be necessary to destroy this one with a hammer.

All these works are no more, in our eyes, than metamorphoses of the bull itself. Over all of them its black shadow falls majestically. One one, *Woman with Hat,* 1942, the horned beast is in the open. Fused with the face of a great lady, dark-grey, rigid, haughty, grave, wearing a veil; one eye energetic, ferocious, and the other more enigmatic, more cloaked; from the wide-brimmed hat two pointed, short horns protrude; two faces in one. A profound seriousness animates the composition; the colors, too, are severe, in consonance with a hieroglyphic which is also strict. How does Picasso achieve this effect? For there is something profoundly mysterious and inaccessible about it.

The bull is the supreme majesty of his art. And all these figures have something about them which suggests they were done in the presence of the bull, that is to say, cruelty, brutality, the dark shadow, the malaise which weighs upon our time, the profound sickness which he must represent, once he determined to undertake this task.

His early canvas *Mother and Child,* 1907, represents an unhappy mother with traces of bountifulness about her, and still careful of her person; a deep anguish, nevertheless, pervades the picture. The child, tiny, degenerated, with a deformed body, hunched shoulders, hairless, decrepit, sick, resembles an old man. The entire composition lives in the soulfulness which escapes through the eyes of these two beings; through their large eyes, open like the eyes which painters of the catacombs or artists in the epoch of Romantic art supplied their figures. But Picasso's brush seems to scratch in the lines, when he draws the marks and scars of suffering, of weeping and pain under those eyes. The painter who has painted them has known how to unmask the bull which is omnipresent in his work. In a book dedicated to Picasso, his long time friend, Jaime Sabartes wrote that from the time of the first brush strokes, Picasso conceived of art as the child of sorrow and pain. The relationship between sorrow and meditation holds good in the same proportion between life and pain, according to the painter. From that time forward, the art of Picasso has shown us sombre tones and traces of desperation in continuing variety.

In *Weeping Woman* Picasso portrays a truly desperate woman; an everyday woman whom we see on the street any day; she wears a modish hat, an embroidered blouse, she might have been shopping, she has brilliantine in her hair; she is a woman whose life at this moment consists in using a handkerchief; she has clearly not been frightened by a horror movie, nor does she cry over a deep-seated cancer which is gnawing at her; her tears remain on her face as if they were distilled there; her eyes do not see beyond her tears; her cheeks and her forehead are joined in their sorrowing expression; her fingers act automatically; all she has left is her handkerchief, the rest is desperation, without a ray of light, without hope. Picasso does not show us anything or hint at anything beyond the shadow of the bull; nothing has dominion in his art but this, so that this woman can think of nothing but her miserable fate; her pain does not have the silent grandeur of simple resignation; she knows nothing of how to endure, she is not able to overcome herself.

And yet, Picasso does not always paint in this way. Many of his figures and many of his canvases possess an unmistakable beauty, a beauty of the most classic kind, as successful and pure as any in contemporary painting. It is interesting to speculate on his predeliction, during either the "blue," "rose," or "white" period, toward painting sleeping figures and mothers with children, as if he deliberately chose subjects living apart from and outside the life of the century, subjects oblivious to worldly events and far from the ire of the bull: the newborn are still unconscious, the sleepers are without care. Consider, on the other hand, the sorrow, the melancholy which Picasso injects into the very marrow of his *saltimbanques* and harlequins, and of his clowns. Subjects of distraction for everyone else, for Picasso the theme provides one more proof of disillusion and bitterness. Think of his bathers: few figures have suffered such a profound commotion as the bathers of Picasso. Perhaps it is because the beach is not merely a nostalgic complex of pure horizons seen through Van Gogh eyes, nor is it altogether the background of bathers *à la* Ingres, nor even simply a place where children play with large and lively-colored balls. The beach is also a place of scheduled and sad discharge; it is also a place of accumulated humanity, nude and disturbing, where all kinds of misfortunes, spiritual as well as physical, are laid bare. Picasso has his targets, his predelictions, his moments, which any reader of Baudelaire will have no trouble in deciphering.

In 1929, Picasso painted the *Young Woman at the Edge of the Sea,* seated in front of the water and sky, raised against the horizon. She envelops the knee of her right leg, which is bent back, with her arms; nothing human surrounds her; the far distance of the horizon, and, perhaps, the very feminine sense of playing a role—this time in the skeletal setting of the end of the world—are somehow sensed; and there is the sense, too, of an immense weariness in the woman's members; the cracking of her bones is the only actual sign of life; there are not even any tears; the flesh has been torn from the jaws, the shoulders droop. The woman lives on alone in the contemplation of a profound disillusion; the pressure of her body against the ground, the folding back upon herself, the erection of the bust, the fleshlessness—which makes her translucent as well as articulated: all this is lively. And yet, it is a skeleton.

All these horrible "figures" of Picasso are not, as we have said before, fantastic. For good reason does their author title them: *Portrait, Portrait with Hat, Portrait with Blue Corsage, Seated Woman, Woman in Armchair.* . . . For they are concrete beings, actual phenomena.

His figures, possessed by the animal, by the mechanistic, signify, in relation to man, a degradation, a fall; a loss of form, of authenticity; a loss of their own identity and being.

It has been said that talent does what it wants, and genius what it must. Picasso's possibilities are endless, no one doubts it. And his painting has about it a sense of duty, of being done because it must.

The horrible ugliness of his figures is not an ugliness of faces, as might be the case if he painted dwarfs, or hideous hags, or monsters. The ugliness of his figures is the ugliness of everyday people living in our midst, the ugliness of our selves; the ugliness of our own souls; the ugliness which is met with and not created arbitrarily. Picasso paints the consequences of our decisions; he paints what is constant in us, in our ugliness. What he paints are quintessences, and not farragos or medleys. And he does so without abandoning the concrete, without recourse to allegory or abstraction.

His figures are not caricatures, and his hieratic forms are beyond the anecdotal or the merely ridiculous situation.

Neither are they masks. They have nothing to do with the quality of Negro masks, or with the masks of the antique world. The new faces of Picasso do not approach us from outside, they are not extrahuman, nor extra-terrestrial spirits. They do not come to meet us, but rather are already within us. And Picasso has revealed a profoundly essential reality: for these figures are a conscious exposition of the Occidental soul.

Whatever else may be said, his art is a return to nature, in a sense that the naturalists themselves did not foresee. It is much more complete than the copyists could imagine, though there are those who foolishly hold that his work is a clever amalgamation of pictures made up in the studios of the primitives and of the old French painting.

A long time had passed since the ceremonial, hieratical manner of working, which was common to religious painting had dissolved into a sentimental way of seeing things and eventuated at last in what was called naturalism, and then later evolved into impressionism. Still later, an art which was closer to the old hieratic art than to naturalism appeared in the Occidental world. Picasso's chosen direction has always been completely clear. He never vacillated. The new "hieraticism," to coin a phrase, is destined to consider, more profoundly than ever before, that man is the living temple of God. Men are not objectified, but are plumbed. The hieraticism of Picasso, nevertheless, contains a chaotic world. He deliberately confuses many beings in one being, just as innocence, tenderness and madness are joined in a single soul—an anarchistic psychology in which noble values are mixed with the most vulgar anti-values. The distinctions which have been scrupulously guarded for centuries and centuries so that they constitute our principal cultural decorum are erased in his work. Sometimes we are tempted to think, as in certain novels, that the protagonist is better the worse he is. But, except for a very few exceptions, Picasso's hieraticism is rooted in the most profound dedication to high moral value.

What, after all, are these "figures" we have been considering: a slap in the face, a sarcasm hurled at the bourgeois world, at liberal hypocrisy, perpetrated with all the acidity and bitterness which is characteristic of Picasso? Or is it true, as some people hold, that only a desperate man could paint such canvases? Or it is not more true that his despair entails a sense of hope?

It is an absurd belief which holds that his figures have focused on women with too-great frequency and that they have done so because of his rage against the entire female sex. If one considers the importance which the female portrait has held in the painting of the past few centuries and the influence it has exerted toward the degradation of pictorial art, Picasso can be seen to be justified. In other epochs of Occidental painting, artists painted the powerful, the hero, the saint without including personal peculiarities of the subject in the hieratic portrait, for individual characteristics tended to disappear in the higher forms which were envisioned. Nowadays the painter does not paint for the Church, or for the King; he paints for whomever will buy, or on commission; in short, for private interests. Feminine beauty has played a role in this process of personalization of art, especially in the liberal art of the nineteenth century. But had Picasso been called upon to paint any of the commissioned paintings of half the museum collections of Europe—and he is a master of the traditional portrait as well—he would doubtlessly have painted them just as he has the figures we have considered above.

Picasso has painted his closest friends, his most beloved friends, sometimes in the traditional classic manner, and then with the most terrible ugliness. The exterior forms are unrelated in large part to the varying state of mind of the painter or of the human model, who is not marble after all, and who changes, or transforms his feelings or beliefs. All the objections that can be imagined against Picasso's art hinge on the following: Is there an art of beauty and another art of expression? There are critics, like Eugenio d'Ors, who ask for the revindication of art as beauty in the face of the new art as expression. And there are others, like Professor Pinder, in Germany, who begins his book *Von den Künsten und der Kunst,* by stating that beauty is not necessary to art but only one of several possible results. In both cases it must be conceded, by both parties, that beauty must be an integral factor, and a deep-seated one, that it must not be merely beauty of the nose, or beauty of the eyes. Beauty as a reflection of deeper truth has had its doors almost hermetically sealed in the painting of recent times—a painting poor in spiritual value—so that it was necessary to open it up, a function which fell in large part to Picasso. It is to his cultivation of the ugly that we devote the following chapter.

Picasso – The Epilogue of the Ugly

IN STUDYING the general history of art, the following division has been postulated: *"l'art pour Dieu," "l'art pour l'art," "l'art pour l'homme."* Picasso's work does not acknowledge any imposed reality; he boasts a complete enmity to pure as well as abstract art. Despite his own objections, for many critics he represents the culmination of the third stage of art as given above. Nevertheless, he is not.

Picasso's work is without direct transcendence toward a higher reality, and yet, his work is eminently transcendental. What remains in his hands retains one of its fundamental dimensions in the spiritual. The qualities proper to his forms do not depend on the subject, as such, nor on any exterior hieratic form, nor on any symbolism. Despite this, we feel that in his painting there is something profoundly enigmatic, super-, or infra-human. In Picasso, man is alone, radically alone, alone with himself. But his art is not humanistic or existentialistic. He paints what he sees and yet his painting is not materialistic. His investigation of man reveals a completely mysterious being, one who flies in the face of all humanistic or scientific presumptions, which are in the end united by a belief in their power to know what constitutes man.

Picasso's art is a new approach to nature. Things recover part of their lost mystery. In any case, the world had been disenchanted too profoundly; spiritual realities were no longer at hand; no secret moved it; man had penetrated everywhere with his technology. But the cracking apart of the humanism of our time brought with it an inclination, a tendency, toward respecting the infallible mystery of things. The ancient world possessed a shadow of this truth, and in some measure this explains Picasso's relation with the classic art of antiquity. His painting—like the philosophy, letters, and the thought of his time—seeks a will without illusions. "Illusionless," Heidegger calls his explanation of existence, a crude and sober knowledge which is characteristic of the works of the epoch.

On the face of it, Picasso seems a profoundly disillusioned man, and in his faces the shine of beauty is interrupted by straight lines.[18] From the birth of his first works this same melancholy or discontent accompanies

[18] *Vide* Walter Erben, *Picasso und die Schwermut,* 1947, p. 25.

his activity. The loss of faith seems to find the most ample expression in his canvases, where the very parts which form the human physiognomy often lose the harmony which physically holds them together. But this does not mean that his art is negative or that his view of the world is negative, any more than Dante could be said to see the world in the manner that he painted Hell. Picasso finds only what he paints.

The preponderance of straight lines in his work over all other lines signifies, among other things, an expression of the mechanical, the rigid, the cold-blooded. The curved line is the true image of life, of the living expression of the idea. The straight line is the line of construction, of discipline, of the cerebral, of intelligence isolated in sensation. It is also the line of opposition. Despite all the talk relative to cubist theses, geometry is to the plastic arts what grammar is to literature. No one interpreted the art of straight lines and rhombs better than Apòllinaire when he defined them as "a necessary evil.' 'It was an art for its time, which was also cold, mechanical, without feeling. "I do not search, I find," is one of the more famous—and not without reason—phrases of Picasso.

Maritain said long ago that cubism could not sustain itself except on the creative force of Picasso. The years have proven this to be terribly true.

Picasso's art has been called the art of doors leading

inward. "Impressionism," wrote Eugenio d'Ors, "had opened the windows to the open air, to nature, to its incessant flux. Picasso closed them once again." A comparison of *The Absinthe Drinker* of Picasso, 1902, and the painting on the same theme by Degas (in the Louvre) clearly demonstrates the significance and range of the interior myth which is in the art of Picasso. What constitutes outward space for the impressionist is for Picasso a turning inward in the face of the dispersing forces of the exterior world. Whether or not the artist made good the promise of a perpetual light shining behind the closed windows, or if on the other hand, he remained in the dark while he went on with his attempts is something left for d'Ors to argue. There are those of us who feel that a great light has been lit on the other side: a light similar to that shining in the chaos surrounding Dostoievsky's construction, or like the light we now discover in the writings of Baudelaire.

Picasso has traveled so far along the highways of the spirit, and in a manner so unusual, that he is able to make landscapes out of the very bodies of humans, and to create an ambient with inanimate things, and transform human physiognomies into backgrounds; he has been able to strangle the closed forms of an object, and, on Euclidean surfaces, and sometimes with bits of eyebrows, mustaches, and with pieces of newspaper, old letters, and shavings, he makes his art serve as a cipher to the spirit and the idea.

There are periods in Picasso, as when he began to cross his canvases with black lines, in which the progressive dissolution of the surface proceeds toward infinity. This tendency, together with others of a related nature led the Marxist critic Max Raphael—who believes that atheism, when it is not based on dialectical materialism, simply substitutes one word for another—to expound the idea that God is the ultimate base of Picasso's art, whether or not the artist is conscious of it.

Thus, it is the judgment of this Marxist that Picasso's negative attitude toward "free thought," his reversion to a medieval ideology, and his psychological dualism, added to the fact that the manifold phantoms of the dead which pullulate in the painter's work are not overcome there, all point to a thoroughly reactionary nature.

Max Raphael therefore relegates the artist to the tradition of Christian Europe, especially because Picasso does not solve the most decisive problem of his ideology, namely the conflict between idealism and materialism. The exaggeration of the two opposing poles, in the judgment of the Marxist critic, demonstrates not only that Picasso's personality is unstable but that it is lacking in any dialectical element. For this reason, Max Raphael feels that Picasso falls within the historic destiny of the bourgeoisie; for the artist's faulty attitude is not due, says Raphael, to any personal capacity, since he is "the best equipped and greatest artist of modern times.' '

One of Picasso's peculiarities, as Christian Zervos has recently shown, is that the preponderance of the spiritual in his work is as essential as is his submission to nature. His work is one that recognizes the precious labor of the spirit, and then grants the rest of the work to nature, with its store of the unexpected; and Picasso has, in this sense, a fidelity to nature which the copyists and naturalists could not have imagined. He does not "paint according to nature, but before her, with her," as one of his own phrases puts it; and in this sentence there is no contradiction, for reality is spirit.

In his *Frontière de la poesie,* Maritain wrote, in relation to Picasso, that art today, as it had during the Renaissance, opens its eyes upon itself, and lives another process of introspection leading to a revolution, as important as the earlier revolution. Maritain considers the terrible progress of Picasso's painting to be equally as important for philosophers as for painters. Painting has advanced one step in its own mystery; tempted and led on by the angelic, one can not say for certain whether at the dictate of a good angel or a demon, especially when considering the concrete case of the painter from Malaga.

In addition to Maritain, Monleon, too, has pointed

out Picasso's faculty for imposing himself on all he touches. The critics speak of his ability to transubstantiate, an ability he has mastered, according to these writers, more through violence than by humility and love. So that the philosopher, more than the artist, says Severini—himself an artist—is better prepared to follow him. And the Italian painter goes on to add that Picasso once told him: "It is the intention which counts."

But if Picasso seems to lose contact with what is seen, it is merely that the same thing is happening to him that happened to Cervantes. The latter is never more profoundly realistic than when he has Don Quixote hoisted on the blades of a windmill. And Picasso is never closer to reality than when he is painting monsters. Nothing is closer to living reality, and yet, his painting is patently moved by an uneasiness which is eminently spiritual. Everything he paints bears an unmistakable imprint, a seal which stamps all his work. It often recalls, in its technique, the hieraticism of medieval art, or the mural paintings of Catalonia. Except for a certain few "standard" productions of the doctrinal cubist period, any canvas of Picasso bears the mark of the forceful personality which could only be Picasso. And yet, he is not a personalist, nor effusive. He goes in search of the ultimate and radical, of a possible permanent reality in the midst of the inexorable flight of time.

He reduces images of appearance to the impalpable,

and reduces mutable structures to something immutable. Behind his plastic forms lies a reality very different from that of the rest of European painting, especially the French, even when identical expressive forms are used.

On the other hand, Picasso's art is eminently historic. It could not be understood outside his time, for history also has its canons. History may be superseded; but it can not be avoided. And it is here that we speak of the duty of genius.

The world of Picasso, besides being enigmatic, mysterious, spiritual, is a world of darkness, a repellent world; and he exposes ugliness itself. Most often his ugliness is without relief; there are works of his, and periods, of an unsuspected and unheard of *lourdeur*. He portrays the animal above the human, the machine above the man. The first impact we receive from Picasso is one of disorder, his profound disorder, which does not have its own consistency, but is disorder in relation to order itself, especially the visible order, that order established by the very nature of things. "*Omne quod manifestatio lumen est,*" (Ephesus V), and the *lumen* made manifest, light in general, is not something which is seen, but that by which something is seen.

Picasso's qualities as an artist show us a creator who considers the world in which we live something more than a place of arbitrary values dependent on the whims and genius of the artist: his constructive discipline, his disdain for all personal effusion in his work, his representation of the essential at the sacrifice of the descriptive, his hatred of copyism, and, though it may sound paradoxical, his contribution toward diffusing a certain taste for simplicity among the public—as can be seen in the influence of his painting reflected in dress decoration, his submission to the given phenomena, all this demonstrates his characteristic soundness. Only in a few instances is it necessary to invoke the excuse that he is experimenting, or that he is Picasso, to pardon some lapse. The metaphysical roots of his art are always in evidence. His dark leap is not the destructive one into the abyss of passion. His work either gives a sign of hope, or when it does not, suggests a secret knowledge, the secret of man as mystery and enigma. Pascal, who also was master of the *gouffre infini,* comes forcibly to mind, with his observations on man, *dans les choses de finesse,* between the two possibilities of being either angel or beast ("what a chimera is man, what an incredible being, what a monster, what a chaos, what a subject of contradictions, what a prodigy"), and then thinking that *l'homme passe infiniment l'homme,* in an infinite process. "The misery of a dispossessed king," was his; and, "whoever will not be an angel, will be a beast." For the world is a mixture of greatness and misery. Something of the same sentiment pervades Picasso, whose figures are sometimes sublime and classic, and at other times are an outpouring of ugliness, an insupportable *tristesse,* as Pascal might say, *le gouffre infini, le moi haissable.*

Another surprising facet of the immense variety of Picasso's dark pathos is his almost pedantic concretion, his sense of the concrete. There is an exact protocol; a fantastic richness in the selection of cruelties and punishments; but his sense of form is replete with a Roman strictness. As in a Dantesque landscape, there is nothing nebulous, nor are there impressionistic asides. A forcefulness of determined judgment is his, clearly and even crudely traced. There are painters of macabre and extravagant taste who, nevertheless, are not masters of the extreme and the ugly on a par with Picasso. The most profound manner of presenting the ugly is to treat it with ugliness, because the artist feels impelled to expose it as ugly and repulsive. And yet, everything true is beautiful, *pulchritudinum ut verum.* In all truth lies beauty.

For those who falsify the relation of art with life, who take refuge in art only in those difficult moments of existence and enjoy it as if it were a fairy story or a dream, for these people Picasso will always remain an unknown. Those who strive to see only one side of life, and this side sublimated or filled with illusion, will never understand Picasso's work. When the paths of the future are confused and tangled, it is precisely then that the true artist can serve as guide and mentor, in the midst of danger as well as in the good fortune of man. Flight, refuge in an art which has from the beginning abdicated all responsibility, is the commodious way out. But to penetrate, as Picasso has, into the region of the black shadows, more is needed than a fortunate artistic formation: the artist must also be far-seeing, a bard, he must feel a profound calling, and possess sufficient courage to battle alone. And yet again, Picasso can not be classified within the mould of any other artist. He is in the line of Pascal, Kierkegaard, Dostoievsky. The closer we approach them, the farther behind the veil they seem to retreat.

It is now more than half a century that the world has occupied itself with Pablo Picasso. He has caused enthusiasm or repulsion, he has attracted or horrified. He stands always within a tempest of applause or of loud protests. No other artist has had so much written about him while still alive. But there is no classifying him. He disconcerts, astonishes, perplexes as he undertakes to open new paths, complicating the way, even for his own partisans. Every ten years, criticism has had to rectify its opinions. At length, everyone has come to an agreement: granted that his work is the terrain of incessant argument, it is also without doubt the terrain of incessant progress, and the history of his art is the history of modern art. Even the dead take on new life in his art.

Wherever he puts his hands, he brings back to life what had appeared to be completely faded and blown, whether it is the dark personages of Toulouse-Lautrec, the heroic mysticism of El Greco, or Oceanic or African sculpture; he helped refurbish the ballet; he provided a more human, more contemporaneous expression to the drawings of Ingres, and he renewed Pompeian painting, classic myth, and the ceramic craft. There is in him no distance which is not measured, no possibility without corresponding attempt. Alongside the strongest abstraction, we find the most concrete object; next to a refined face, the most brutal expression, beside the most extraordinary fright, the most delicate sentiment. And this has been going on for half a century—a half century without possible indifference on the part of the world to his art. Where is the secret of such an extraordinary production? Other contemporary artists have been celebrated, before and after Picasso, and their fame has meanwhile passed away. For Picasso to imprison time as he has done it was not enough to count on the air of newness, of experimentation and perturbation. His power depends on something stronger than what is isolated in his "blue" or "rose" periods, or in his supersentitive brushwork, or in Orphic poetry. Chagall appreciated Picasso, above all else, for his feeling for ornamentation and the arabesque, his *papier collé*. Others have appreciated his Spanish crudity and force modified by French *gaieté*. Eluard, Cassou, and many others have written on his feeling for solitude. Perhaps his vision of the myth of the bull, which we have here presented, may add something to the clarification of the ultimate meaning of his work. In one of his poems Picasso says: "he read the future in the eye of the bull," and he repeats this thought in other versions of his very individual poems. This is his fundamental vision. His visionary painting stands far above other contemporary artists, in the same manner that the poetry of Dante, or Hölderlin, stand above the subjectivist, *"charmant,"* aesthetic poetry of their contemporaries.

There was a time when a critic of the quality of T. S. Eliot—and he himself tells us of it—could not bring himself to read the *Paradiso* of Dante, though he could, and did, read the *Inferno*. Eliot describes this attitude in his study of the Florentine genius, and he explains how it was not until much later that he could enter into the Dantesque Paradise. The epoch which rejected all serene and graceful accent—for this epoch was perhaps tired of a vision in the manner of Dante Rossetti—rejected everything which might appear gentle or mild. Horror of the delicate and the showy developed into a fury against it. In the case of Dante, his interpreters were responsible for a false view of his work. But today, we are already aware that we have suffered a black academicism which was as bad—and as false—as the old rose-colored academicism. "It is just as absurd for the girl in the florist shop to be strangled at the hands of the prince, as it was for her to wind up marrying him." We have grown weary of bitter characters, and of somber, tragic tones without relief. Forty or more odd years of experiment in painting is a long time. Moreover, genius does not negate, destroy, or experiment in an unceasing manner; the function of genius is simply to create. The change is beginning to be noticed: "the cult of the ugly is reaching its end." If Picasso did not furnish it the *coup de grâce,* it is he who carries the dagger for the final thrust. Even Salvador Dalí has taken note of this event, in a statement for the *Correo Literario,* in 1950: "Pablo Picasso is the great demolisher, the most outrageous and greatest demolisher of the century. In a recent letter which I addressed him from Spain, I thanked him for having assassinated official painting and modern painting as well. After him, nothing remains to be done. He has left behind no path along which to carry on his work." It is possible to feel as Eugenio d'Ors does, that Picasso has not justified the early hopes placed in him—but then d'Ors had taken the early Picasso to be another Raphael. In truth, no man can continue wrapped up in himself as a self-contained reality: he exists insofar as he goes out to the encounter, the encounter with something which speaks to him, elevates him; if he does not do this, he fails, and his terrible and absolute solitude is seen to be insupportable. And yet Picasso has attempted to paint man in his solitude, and he has understood him better than anyone else in our time understood him in his complete anguish, his most profound and radical aloneness. Once again Pascal comes to mind: "If man is great by nature and petty by fault, his greatness consists, then, in acknowledging his pettiness." And it is the plastic understanding of the tragic weakness which makes the work of Picasso great.

Those of us who believe that art should reflect in some way the nostalgia for a full life, a life which we do not in truth possess, but which despite all disillusion we know must exist as we imagine it, can be especially gratified with the later objectives which seem to lie behind Picasso's creation. The long period of extreme nervous tension which found its sharpest expression in *Guernica* and the *Skull of a Bull on a Table* was followed by a lyric *intermezzò*, which saw the production of an important group of drawings of ardent pastorals, a vibrant and passionate expansion of an instinct which seemed outside the orbit of the corrida.

The 1946 pastoral in the Antibes Museum, a great composition which sums up all his drawing of that period, is an outburst of life, joy and fecundity, of sympathy for man, for the palpitations of his heart, a strong compound of classicism and sound primitivism.

His store of poetic sensibility, charged with a sense of natural phenomena, allows us to see in Picasso an added quality as mythologist of a world desired by all humanity.

In the final analysis, the spirituality of Picasso, his attack on bourgeois values, his "black painting," may constitute nothing less than the proposed liquidation of an art, several centuries old now, which is best described as secularized or paganized, and which had its origin about 1500. Art, which was formerly in the service of gods and the service of primitive religions, in the service of the king, or of a saint, retained even through the middle ages the lordliness of its hieratic forms. Little by little, forms which were all-too-human began to appear and turned idealized images into vulgar ones, leaving us the forms with which we are now most familiar and against which Picasso seems to struggle: bourgeois and individualized art, where consideration is given only what is seen with the eyes of the flesh. In later times, great artists have had to find the bases for their great art within themselves, the outer source having been lost and dispersed. Rembrandt is the best example of this isolated artist; before him Michaelangelo, and after him, Beethoven. The personal value of these artists, their monumental conceptions, were pardoned them as giants, but the same liberties seemed dangerous for the ordinary to risk. Speaking of these matters, Pinder[10] criticizes the point of view of those (and he cites Ortega y Gasset) who, in an attemmpt to relieve modern art of its deadly heaviness, borne down by the too-human elements which have been in the ascendant since romantic naturalism, imagine and advocate a more joyful art. Against the opinion of these critics to the effect that art is born of the instinct for play, Pinder counterposes an opinion he believes rooted in history, and holds that an art based on play would have evolved into something unfortunate. Modern art is often the very opposite of play, its accent being on the solitary, and even on the despairing. In all times art has been equivalent to service, at least in all periods of strength. Art does not so much need friends and lovers, connoisseurs and critics, as it does those who will accept it with veneration and respect. Neither art nor artists have ever offered the solution which religion has, as Pinder points out. Picasso's religion is the religion of the centaurs, fauns, satyrs, bulls. His is the classic manner of approaching noumenal concepts. Picasso's vision is enigmatic, mysterious. His anti-bourgeois feeling, his hatred of personal expatiation, his profound respect amid much apparent irreverence, all help to open doors long closed to contemporary sensibility. The truth is that, modern as he may be, man does not cease

[10] Pinder, *Von den Künsten und der Kunst*, p. 75.

to be a religious animal; but, without God, his obsession focuses on substitutes. It is not enough to paint the dark forces of evil. The greatest art will be that which, taking anguish as its point of departure, will triumph over it and give man confidence in his power and salvation.

Still, the dawn of classical mythology, it has been said, rises from the blood of a dead bull.

The Fiesta

FINALLY, it should prove of interest to relate Picasso's vision of the bulls to their festive characteristic. In this connection we must begin with the following question: Is the running of the bulls a true festival? A festival is more than a day of celebration and merry-making; it is not an isolated revelry; it is more, even, than the communal unconscious, liberated and expressive of racial and occult impulses. Nor is it something merely edifying or instructive. The true festival, the *fiesta,* must have a basic significance, an authentic life, a capacity which is not merely the result of human promotion. Every true festival requires a higher initiative. The true festival—and this has been the same in all epochs—can only exist where the gods, the divinities lend their presence. It is the privilege only of sound, believing peoples to express themselves in common, well-defined and harmonious festivals.

Not all civilized peoples have festivals, and many of the fetes and festivals that do exist among civilized people are not true festivals. Many of them recall the Jacobin savor of the numberless fetes which Robespierre tried to establish by decree in 1794—as if festivals could be instituted by a stroke of the pen—, such as the Festival of the Human Race, the Festival of Agriculture, the Festival of Youth, the Festival of Liberty, of Beneficence, of the Sovereignty of the People, of Crafts, of Equality, of the Republic, of Truth, of Justice, of Hatred of Tyrants and Traitors, of Conjugal Love. In those days the Goddess Reason was paraded through the streets to her Temple. These festivals were ephemeral and rachitic and lasted as long as the regime which established them. Some other peoples have not yet found their festive expression. They have to contract with the Negro for their happiness: and so they hire noise and jazz-bands.

True festivals, the *fiesta,* find their inspiration in the sphere of the fascinating, the divine, the overpowering, and bear the mark of the hope that is most profound in the human imagination; so that there is always a powerful and mysterious element in these celebrations which escapes analysis; and this was true of the classic festivals of the Greeks, the Romans, the Jews. The last-mentioned first introduced the historic festivals, where the date played the part which Nature played in the festivals of the other nations. But just as much in one nation as in the others, the appearance and deeds of God and of the gods were the events celebrated. Then came the diversions: to divert oneself signifies to turn aside, to separate oneself from others. What one really does is separate *out* one's own person so as to merge with all other men on the basis of what we all have in common. Men can think differently, they can have different ideas, but when they are *en fête,* diverting themselves, the same thing happens to them that happens to mountains: they are all joined at their base. And what one has in common with other men are never thoughts or ideas, but beliefs; they are our common bond. It is for this reason that festivals are necessarily popular. The true festival has always had a religious fundament, for the simple reason that wherever public joy reaches its maximum limit, just as whenever sorrow goes beyond ordinary bounds, there religion enters the scene. In short, festivals can not be created by decree, nor do they come about by themselves. They celebrate divinities. The Spanish Catholic liturgy is magnificent in this way, for every day is *fiesta.* There are so many *fiestas* in the Spanish Church that it has become necessary to limit the lesser in the interests of the larger celebrations. But, in truth, for the profoundly religious, the entire year is a year of *fiesta.*

In our time one has the feeling that festivals have lost their religious attribute, and that they are connected with gods who have departed, with divinities sinking beneath the waves, and that everything is lost, not only from impiety but also in weak didactic and edifying talk. Our epoch, eminently irreligious, is a time of revelry and not of festival. One need only compare a modern carnival, with its harlequins, pierrots, and confetti, with the vigor and force still retained in the old carnival of some regions of South Germany, at Elsach, in Baden, for instance. The unity and common bases which formerly "diverted" men have been steadily losing their power; for this reason festivals have fallen into decline and lost their value, to such a point that one wants to cry out with the poet:

> I should like to be festive—but why?
> And I should like to sing with the others:
> but I'm so much alone that I lack
> the divine force.
>
> *(Menons Klagen und Diotima)*

And this same poet, Friedrich Hölderlin, says in other lines, after turning away from the sight of his suffering contemporaries:

> Our lineage
> lives as in Hell
> without divinity, occupied only in enterprise:

each one listening to himself alone in the workshop
where barbarians work with thick arms
without rest: but, for all the enterprise,
there is no fruit
but only the Furies, and wretched effort.

(Der Archipielagus)

In the corrida one thing is indisputably evident: the Spanish are in *fiesta.* It is, in fact, the national *fiesta.* As we have been pointing out this indisputable characteristic is to be explained only because of the residue of ancient mythic belief, animating a spectacle which arouses the memory of great and fascinating deeds, and that this representation is enriched by Christian belief as well.

Up until only a short time ago, as Don Ramó Pérez de Ayala points out in his book *Política y toros,* the bullfighting season was inaugurated each year in Spain with great solemnity on Easter Sunday, the Sunday of Resurrection. This was a liturgical day, in the cult of the bull as well as in the Catholic ritual. With anxious hearts the populace waited through the forty days of Lent for the advent of the glorious and luminous day. Before the traditionally appointed date, the impresarios would not have dared to organize or announce corridas, nor the toreros to have fought the bulls, nor the public to have watched them. Edmund de Amicis, in his book, *Voyages in Spain,* describes the anxiety and impatience of the

Spanish as they waited the inauguration of the season. The first to fight bulls during Lent was Bombita, in the last year of his public life. Pérez de Ayala makes the following significant commentary about this innovation: "It is worth noting this date with the most detailed attention, because it is of the greatest importance for future investigators in the history of Spain, a country where only one other kind of building exceeds in number the *plazas de toros*—and that is the religious edifices, the convents."

Richard Ford, the English author of *Gatherings from Spain,* only fully realized he was no longer in England when he watched the populace pour out to the corrida. He described the phenomenon in an article, which a little later became part of his famous book, in the following manner: " . . . All the world crowds to the *Plaza de toros.* You need not ask the way; just launch into the tide, which in these Spanish affairs will assuredly carry you away. Nothing can exceed the gaiety and sparkle of a Spanish public going, eager and full-dressed, to the *fight.* They could not move faster were they running away from a real one. All the streets or open spaces near the outside of the arena present of themselves a spectacle to the stranger, and genuine Spain is far better to be seen and studied in the streets, than in the saloon. Now indeed a traveller from Belgravia feels that he is out of town, in a new world and no mistake; all around him is a perfect saturnalia, all ranks are fused in one stream of living beings, one bloody thought beats in every heart, one heart beats in ten thousand bosoms; every other business is at an end, the lover leaves his mistress unless she will go with him,—the doctor and lawyer renounce patients, briefs, and fees; the city of sleepers is awakened, and all is life, noise, and movement, where tomorrow will be the stillness and silence of death; now the bending line of the *Calle de Alcalá,* which on other days is broad and dull as Portland Place, becomes the aorta of Madrid, and is scarcely wide enough for the increased circulation; now it is filled with a dense mass coloured as the rainbow, which winds along like a spotted snake to its prey. Oh the din and dust! The merry mob is everything, and like the Greek chorus, is always on the scene. How national and Spanish are the dresses of the lower classes—for their betters alone appear like Boulevard quizzes, or tigers cut out from our East end tailors' pattern-book of the last new fashion; what *Manolas,* what reds and yellows, what fringes and flounces, what swarms of picturesque vagabonds, cluster, or alas, clustered, around *calesas,* whose wild drivers run on foot, whipping, screaming, swearing; the type of these vehicles in form and color was Neapolitan; they alas! are also soon destined to be sacrificed to civilization to the 'bus and common-place cab, or vile fly.

"The *plaza* is the focus of a fire, which blood alone can

extinguish; what public meetings and dinners are to Britons, reviews and razzias to Gauls, mass or music to Italians, is this one and absorbing bullfight to Spaniards of all ranks, sexes, ages, for their happiness is quite catching; and yet a thorn peeps amid these rosebuds; when the dazzling glare and fierce African sun calcining the heavens and earth, fires up man and beast to madness, a raging thirst for blood is seen in flashing eyes and the irritable ready knife, then the passion of the Arab triumphs over the coldness of the Goth: the excitement would be terrific were it not on pleasure bent; indeed there is no sacrifice, even of chastity, no denial, even of dinner, which they will not undergo to save money for the bull-fight."

The article drew attention in the literary circles of London in 1820. A publisher summoned the then-unknown Ford and commissioned him to write a book of voyages regarding Spain, and that is how the famous chronicle, *Gatherings From Spain,* came about.

This festive character of the corrida, both profound and brilliant, makes all the more absurd certain modern attempts to bring into relation the somber lowing of the bull, riddled with pain, with the new international taste for sport; attempts in this direction have proven dismal failures in Spain. In the first place, the over-all assumption is that sport is a clean, beautiful endeavor, while the old rite is something violent, impassioned and tragic. An attempt has been made to relate the horse in the corrida to its role in the circus—by way of equating it to the horse of imaginary Far West cowboys. It may not be a bad idea to vindicate the role of the horse in the corrida, but from there to introduce the concepts of sport into something so totally different as the world of the corrida is an inadmissible notion. It would, of course, constitute a weakening of the black legend of Spain, if this watering of the corrida were to come about, and it would be a new—if false—link between the Hispanic and Anglo-Saxon worlds, but for all of that it would be inadmissible. The countries which dominate always impose their customs and games, and for this reason the Spanish corrida has more than once been on the point of disappearance in the face of an international sanction initiated by the Anglo-Saxon nations amid tearful cries from the pro-animal societies. At last, the disemboweled horses have been dispensed with in the corrida and their place taken by padded ones; in exchange the participants are granted the privilege of appearing in technicolor in the movie palaces of the world. Recently, the Americans (who in their own country do not shudder at erecting stands to watch all manner of brutality, from endurance dances to the head-on crash of two locomotives) have come to Spain to organize, at Montjuich Stadium in Barcelona, an auto-rodeo, in regard to which we will forebear making the remarks such a move deserves: suffice it to say that this kind of spectacle can scarcely make a favorable impression in Spain, where the taxis in use on the public streets are older than the automobiles the Americans burn up in their spectacles.

This is not the place to discuss sport, about which some statements have recently appeared in Europe that even its apologists have not answered. In any case, let Spain conserve the pure character of the corrida, that bath of youth, which as Barres said, "belongs to the youngest youth, and which comes from animality."

The bulls of Picasso, however, do not pertain to the Spanish *fiesta*. The *fiesta* makes no appearance in his art. His *Pastoral* is merely a spark of what could be the joyful bonfire lit by the hands of an artist of his caliber. But the *fiesta* turned to water in his art one "bad afternoon," on the bad afternoon of the West; and from the century's sea of folly emerges a black bull which remains to be fought. Around the black bull, heaped about with gold, dance the vulgar and the gross in the manner of their liturgy. This minotaur is a complex one, with its outer and inner Furies, let loose on a desolate and frightened world. The bull stands alone, tragically alone. But its victory is simultaneous with its defeat. Though it may attempt suicide in the moment of desperation, it must live on, eternally damned, and condemned to live in solitude, in the solitude of eternity, just as we have felt it throughout the history of humanity. It will not join either God or man. And its solitude will never end.

> Still, what difference does it make
> whether the thief of Europe
> triumphs in deceit, if the sun of Spain
> flashes the first ray?

Thus sang Calderón in another century. And only in this spirit can the *fiesta* be triumphant.

Vade retro, Satanás!

GLOSSARY

Because English equivalents for Spanish terms in the so-called "bullfight" are in most cases inaccurate, the Spanish has been used wherever feasible. The most readily available Spanish-English dictionaries are inadequate: the largest, Valázquez, for instance, is absurd.

aficionado: a serious devotee (of the "bullfight" in the present context); the designation presupposes some knowledge on the part of the person described (often a weighty pedantry in the world of the bulls), but also assumes that the person is an amateur and not a professional.

corrida: there is no Spanish original for the English "bullfight"; therefore, we have not striven to impose this English word on the text, and have used it only when the Spanish name for the same thing would be unwieldy or unnecessary; the term "bullfight" is a makeshift word for corrida, or more fully *corrida de toros,* literally, the running of the bulls; since this literal translation is somewhat awkward, it is used sparingly in this translation, while corrida is often (but not always) left untranslated, especially where the ritual-spectacle in its full sense is meant; a satisfactory discussion of the tripartite corrida, with its strict divisions and rules, will be found in many recent books on the subject; there is an amazing amount of balderdash written about the corrida, and most encyclopedia articles, for instance, where one would expect some objectivity, are laughable (the entry in the English *Everyman's* 12-volume set, as an example, under "bullfight," was apparently written by an SPCA official and is ludicrously false—the bull is said to be "led out," etc.; the *Columbia Viking Desk Encyclopedia* explains that the matador "is assisted by *banderilleros,* who enrage bulls by stabbing them with darts, *picadores* who jab bulls with lances, and *toreros* who distract bulls by waving red flags": a semi-criminal description of some writer's dream of the corrida); an article by the noted Spanish author José Maria Gironella, however, in the latest revised *American Peoples Encyclopedia* gives an accurate and objective account of the modern corrida.

fiesta: in Spain, *la fiesta nacional,* or even more simply, *nuestra fiesta* (our *fiesta)* means the bullfight; the last section of the present book deals with the *fiesta* as a whole, but elsewhere in the text, *fiesta* most usually means the *fiesta* par excellence, and not merely a parochial fete.

plaza de toros: the bullring, also called, in Spanish, *coso.*

tauromachia: from *taurus,* bull, and *machia,* (Greek *maché*) battle.

PICASSO

and the BULL